Innovative Classroom Practices Using ICT in England

Sue Harris

Alison Kington

Published in November 2002
by the National Foundation for Educational Research,
The Mere, Upton Park, Slough, Berkshire SL1 2DQ

ISBN 1 903880 35 1

CONTENTS

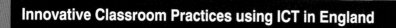

Innovative Classroom Practices using ICT in England

ACKNOWLEDGEMENTS

We would like to express our thanks to all those who have contributed to the data collection, analysis and reporting which forms the basis for this national report:

- the teachers and headteachers, students and their parents, and LEA staff who gave freely of their time during our data collection
- members of the National Steering Group for their assistance and guidance throughout the course of the study
- Seamus Hegarty, Director of NFER, for his support for the project
- Robert Kozma, the international study director based at SRI International, California and colleagues in other countries who contributed to the international effort
- Barbara Lee, Marilyn Leask and Sunita Bhabra, who formed part of the national research team
- Peter Rudd and Ruth Carim, for their helpful comments on the draft report
- Pauline Pearce and Effie Sudell for providing secretarial assistance
- Mary Hargreaves, who prepared the layout, Nicolle Thomas, who designed the cover, and Wendy Tury, who coordinated the publication of the report.

Finally, we are grateful to the schools and parents who granted permission for photographs of students involved in the innovations to be included in this report.

RESEARCH SUMMARY

The Second Information Technology in Education Study (SITES) was organised by the International Association for the Evaluation of Educational Achievement (IEA) and was designed to collect and disseminate information about the use of information and communication technologies (ICT) in schools. Part of the study was concerned with collecting data concerning innovative pedagogical practices using ICT by means of qualitative methods: case studies within schools. Importantly, national research centres were directed by the study coordinators to select examples of innovative practices using technology, as opposed to examples of practices using innovative technology. This selection criterion was intended to ensure that the practices studied had a high chance of being sustained in the original institutions and also of being transferred into other institutions. England was one of more than 40 countries that participated in this aspect of the SITES research.

Within England, six different innovations were studied: three within primary schools and three within secondary schools. The innovations within primary schools were:

♦ All-day access to their own PC for each pupil in Year 6

♦ Writing for a real purpose: communication by email between ten-year-olds and employees at a mobile phone factory

♦ Challenge 2000: an internet-based resource for stimulating cooperative group work with a focus on cross-curricular research, problem-solving and cultural awareness in Year 6.

The innovations within secondary schools were:

♦ 'Turning potential into performance': using a database to record, monitor and set targets for student performance throughout a secondary school

♦ A two-year on-line course leading to accreditation in ICT at 16+

♦ Using video-conferencing to improve English students' conversational skills in French in Year 11.

The research involved interviews with school staff, students and parents together with examination of school documents and observations of lessons. Collectively, the case studies revealed a number of positive impacts on the students that participated in the innovations, including:

♦ Improved motivation

♦ Improved presentation of work, as a result of using ICT more

♦ Increased ability to work independently

♦ Increased ability to organise their own work (i.e. prioritise)

- ◆ Enhanced social skills/confidence in communicating with others outside their school and family circles

- ◆ Increased confidence, self-esteem and self-discipline

- ◆ Improved attendance at school

- ◆ Improved group working and cooperative skills

- ◆ Improved ICT skills

- ◆ Increased responsibility for their own learning, which was seen as useful preparation for further study in secondary school/further education/ higher education.

The teachers involved in the innovative practices in both primary and secondary schools reported that their classroom practice had become less didactic and their role within the classroom had become more that of a guide or facilitator, able to offer one-to-one support to individual students as required.

Although the practices within the six schools were very different, they illustrate two main ways in which classroom practice can change as a result of utilising ICT:

- ◆ Involving others outside the physical classroom in learning/social activities

- ◆ Changing interactions within the classroom.

CHAPTER 1: INTRODUCTION

1.1 Background

In England, there is substantial government commitment to ICT for all, not only through primary, secondary, further and higher education, but also as a mechanism for lifelong learning. Numerous initiatives signal the importance of ICT to teaching and learning, including: investment in ICT resources for schools; the establishment of ICT as a core subject within the National Curriculum; the ongoing development of the National Grid for Learning (NGfL); a National Curriculum for initial teacher training institutions for the use of ICT for subject teaching; in-service professional development in ICT skills for teachers and librarians through New Opportunities Fund (NOF) training; and financial support for teachers to purchase their own computers through Computers for Teachers and Laptops for Teachers. These initiatives at national and school levels are intended to encourage teachers to increase their use of ICT within their classroom practice, as well as enhancing their confidence and skills in using ICT.

The use of ICT within the classroom offers opportunities for new approaches to teaching and learning, extending the learning environment beyond the classroom and allowing students to communicate with adults other than their teachers and family members. With these new opportunities in mind, the International Association for the Evaluation of Educational Achievement (IEA) set up a major international research study designed to collect detailed information about ICT practices in schools in the participating countries: the Second Information Technology in Education Study (SITES). The project has three separate modules:

Modules

- **Module 1** (1997–99): a quantitative phase, with a survey of ICT in schools by means of questionnaires sent to headteachers and heads of ICT/ICT coordinators;

- **Module 2** (1999–2002): a qualitative phase, with case studies of innovative pedagogical practices in schools;

- **Module 3** (2002–05): a quantitative phase, with surveys for students and teachers, plus an optional Performance Assessment component for students.

The first module of the SITES project involved collection of quantitative data; England did not participate in that part of the study, although about 30 countries were involved. The second module of the study was concerned with the collection of qualitative data, and focused specifically on innovative pedagogical practices using technology (summarised as 'innovations'). Countries that did not take part in Module 1 were not barred from participation in Module 2, and England was one of the countries involved in this component of the study. The national research was carried out by the National Foundation for Educational Research (NFER) and was funded jointly by NFER and the Department for Education and Skills (DfES). This report presents background information about the aims of the SITES Module 2 research, the methods used to collect data, and findings from the case studies carried out in schools in England.

1.2   SITES M2 aims

The main aims of the international research included:

Main aims

- ◆ to identify and describe innovative pedagogical practices that use technology;
- ◆ to inform practices related to ICT;
- ◆ to provide teachers and other practitioners with information that they can use to improve classroom practices;
- ◆ to add to the body of research knowledge and theory about the factors across countries that contribute to the successful and sustained use of innovative technology-based pedagogical practices.

More specifically, the data collection was intended to provide evidence to answer the following research questions:

Research questions

- ◆ What are the innovative pedagogical practices in which teachers use ICT? Why are they working?
- ◆ How do these practices change what teachers do in the classroom?
- ◆ How do these innovations change what students do in the classroom?
- ◆ What impact do these practices have on student outcomes? How have they changed the way outcomes are assessed?
- ◆ Which national and school policies related to staff development, Internet access etc., are potentially effective in supporting these innovations?

The research in England involved case studies carried out in three primary and three secondary schools during the school year ending July 2001. The six schools were selected on the basis of an innovative practice established within the school that seemed to have a beneficial impact on students (in terms of achievement, attitudes, motivation and/or behaviour), and which showed potential for being sustained over time and being transferred into other year groups and/or other schools. Summary information about how the study was carried out is presented in section 1.3 below. The national research team submitted a report on each school to the international coordinators.

Together with the national reports submitted by other countries, the full case reports from England will be available via the Internet (see http://sitesm2.org). The study coordinators (the International Coordinating Committee – ICC) will carry out cross-national analyses on the reports submitted by England and the other countries participating in the study so as to identify main themes emerging from all cases (approximately 170 in total): their analyses will form the basis for an international report.

1.3   Methodology

A national panel representing policy makers, ICT specialists and teacher trainers drew up a shortlist of potential schools to be the subject of case studies. Selection criteria included: innovative classroom practices that utilised ICT; evidence of improving standards; levels of resources which could be achieved by other schools; and a favourable OFSTED report. The research team visited all the shortlisted schools to confirm their suitability and willingness to participate. The team submitted eight nominations of innovative practices to the international coordinators, and six were accepted.

The case studies in each of the schools involved collecting data by means of interviews, observations, surveys of headteachers and ICT coordinators/heads of ICT and collecting relevant documents (such as ICT policies and school development plans) for analysis. The research team worked within each school for a period of five days.

More detailed information about methodology is presented in Appendix I.

1.4   This report

This report presents findings from the six SITES case studies carried out in England. Chapter 2 summarises the initiatives and policies that form the national context for the research, and outlines the innovations in each school: in accordance with international guidelines, the names of all schools mentioned in this report have been changed to preserve anonymity. Chapter 3 identifies main themes emerging from the six cases in England, highlights the implications for schools and suggests points that schools may consider before amending their own practices. Finally, Chapter 4 presents detailed information about the six different innovations.

CHAPTER 2: NATIONAL AND INDIVIDUAL CONTEXTS FOR THE CASE STUDIES IN ENGLAND

This chapter outlines the national context for the SITES M2 case studies carried out in England during the 2000–01 school year, and summarises the innovations studied in each school, which in turn relate to the national and/or local policies and initiatives.

2.1 National contexts

At the time of data collection, practices in schools were influenced by a number of government programmes, policies and targets, some of which were directly related to information and communications technology (ICT) and some of which were more general.

A main concern was to increase ICT skills, not only for students[1] who would start their working careers in the twenty-first century, but also for practising teachers in all subjects and phases of education.

Government targets for the year 2002 as outlined in national initiatives, include:

Government targets

- ◆ Teachers should be confident and competent in teaching using ICT across the curriculum. A main mechanism for achieving this is the New Opportunities Fund (NOF) training for teachers and librarians; this scheme utilises funds raised by the national lottery to support projects in education, health and the environment. Under this scheme, schools have to plan and implement programmes of in-service training with the aim of raising the skills levels of all teachers, rather than just ICT specialists.

- ◆ All schools should be connected to the Internet; within England, the National Grid for Learning (NGfL) represents both a means of accessing information (connectivity) and the numerous resources available (content) to support education and lifelong learning.

- ◆ Most school leavers should be competent in ICT and there should be measures in place for assessing their ICT skills. Importantly, accreditation in ICT should be achieved by the majority of school leavers, rather than just those who choose to specialise in ICT. In addition to the accreditation options for students at age 16, the Key Skills programme, in operation from September 2000, offers post-16 students the opportunity to work towards accreditation in ICT, either in combination with other skills (communication and application of number), or on its own.

---

[1] Within this report the term 'students' is used to refer to all young people in schools. When referring to practices in specific primary schools, the term 'pupils' is used.

An additional means of raising teachers' ICT skills was established in the Computers for Teachers initiative (now superseded by Laptops for Teachers[2]), which offered a grant to assist teachers who wanted to purchase their own computer to support their professional activities. The scheme was introduced in 2000, and a condition of the scheme was that teachers must participate in NOF training (newly qualified teachers who had covered ICT as a mandatory part of their training were exempt from this requirement).

Another initiative involving teachers was the creation of Advanced Skills Teacher status, which entails the award of additional funds to teachers with particular skills. Teachers with Advanced Skills status work within their own school and with teachers in other schools to share their expertise in specific curriculum areas, for example biology or ICT.

Practices in schools were also influenced by two further factors: firstly, the introduction of the National Literacy Strategy and the National Numeracy Strategy into primary schools, as part of a general concern to raise standards of achievement; and secondly, the established policy of teaching students with special educational needs within mainstream schools wherever possible.

Finally, the government is keen to encourage working adults to offer support and encouragement to young people by becoming mentors. In addition to providing insights into the world of adult work, contact with mentors is seen as a way of renewing the motivation of disaffected young people who may be under-performing in the traditional classroom situation[3].

2.2 The individual school innovations and their contexts

2.2.1 Primary 1

Windmill Primary School had a high percentage of pupils with special educational needs: the school prided itself on accepting pupils who had been excluded from other schools. The school had a strong ethos of encouraging all pupils to fulfil their potential, and in its prospectus expressed its aims as to

> ...empower all pupils to be better able to be in control of their own learning and lives, and to be better able to act with rationality, sensitivity and humanity. Among its priorities, the school intends to ensure that the curriculum, as expressed in terms of objectives, is resourced at an appropriate level to ensure that breadth, depth and balance are established and sustained.

Accordingly, as part of its strategies towards fulfilling these aims, the school had equipped all 46 pupils in Year 6 with their own desktop computer. Pupils had all-day access to their PC, including Internet access, and were able to use their machine for any aspect of their work.

---

[2] See http://lft.ngfl.gov.uk/.

[3] See http://www.dfes.gov.uk/a-z/MENTORING_ba.html.

2.2.2   Primary 2

Woodford Junior School was situated in a deprived area, with many single-parent families and approximately 44 per cent of pupils entitled to free school meals. The school ICT coordinator explained, *'Parents don't work, own a computer, or have contact with other people.'* Consequently, the school staff were concerned that many pupils had no role model of a working parent, and the aspirations for pupils' future education were very low, largely because their families had had very poor experiences of education. Part of the school vision was to create a computer literate society, not only for pupils at the school, but also for the wider community, so the school purchased 40 laptop computers which pupils in Years 4, 5 and 6 could use at school and also take home, thereby extending the experiences with ICT to pupils' families. A further initiative (and the one which the SITES case study focused on) was designed to improve the communication skills of pupils and raise their aspirations by pairing selected children in Year 5 with volunteer employees at the nearby Ericsson mobile phone company. The partners were termed 'epals' because communication with them took place by email.

2.2.3   Primary 3

Moorcroft Primary School was a popular school in an urban area; the local education authority (LEA) had been given Pathfinder status in 1998 as part of the National Grid for Learning initiative. There were 40–50 children with two teachers in each year group, and, due to the physical constraints of the building, the school implemented a team-teaching approach in each year group, rather than splitting the children into two parallel classes. The school had a strong history of being involved in innovations in ICT and chose this as a means of marking the new millennium: the ICT coordinator designed a cross-curricular resource to encourage pupils to search for information via the Internet. The work, named Challenge 2000, was set in the context of a journey around the world in a hot air balloon, with monthly challenges, divided into stages which had to be achieved in order to continue the journey.

2.2.4   Secondary 1

Highgrove High School was a large co-educational secondary school with approximately 1900 students aged 11–18 years. The students came from a variety of backgrounds, but most continued their education into the sixth form (the school had approximately 400 in the sixth form) with 60 per cent of the 11-plus cohort going on to university. The school collected data about students' performance in standardised tests, National Curriculum Assessments and ongoing work in all subjects and used these to set targets for students. Due to the large number on roll, the staff realised that ICT would simplify the task of recording and monitoring all the data they collected, and had chosen a database which would run on the school's mixed platform of Macs and PCs: Claris Filemaker. The careful monitoring of individual students' performance across all subjects throughout the school enabled teachers to identify students whom they thought were underachieving, and target these for additional attention and support. The move from using the performance data summatively to formatively, setting targets for pupils, was widely attributed to be one of the reasons for the substantial improvement in the school's examination results.

2.2.5   Secondary 2

Coleridge College was a large technology college covering the 14–19 age range. It was one of a number of secondary schools approached by Walton High School (another technology college) towards the end of the 1999–2000 school year, with the offer to supply the materials to run an on-line intermediate GNVQ in ICT for an annual fee. The course materials had been prepared by staff at Walton High School in accordance with the Oxford Cambridge and RSA Examinations (OCR[4]) syllabus requirements, and was promoted as being equivalent to four GCSE passes at grades A*–C. Coleridge College decided to run the course as an after-school option offered to the new intake of Year 10 students, partly because it was seen as a way of helping to raise the performance of students who were likely to achieve fewer than five GCSE passes at grades A*–C, but also because staff felt that the difference in the method of course delivery would be an attraction for demotivated students, and it would enable students who had not elected to study ICT at GCSE level to extend their knowledge and skills in ICT.

2.2.6   Secondary 3

Belgrove High School had specialist status as a language college, and had approximately 800 students aged 13–18 years on roll. The college was well equipped with ICT resources, having 76 networked PCs in a central, pyramid-shaped study centre, a further 25 machines in an adjacent annexe for modern foreign languages, a suite of 30 machines in the mathematics department and 12 computers in the sixth-form study room. The policy throughout the modern foreign languages (MFL) department was that one in every five lessons must be ICT-based, either in the pyramid or the annexe. The school first became involved in links with schools in other EU countries as part of the Education Department's Superhighways Initiative through the Students Across Europe project which aimed to implement new forms of language teaching and learning in French, German and Spanish, based on peer-group tutoring and the use of multimedia resources to supplement traditional teaching. A follow-up project, Students Across Europe Language Network, was conceived to run from 1996 to 1999 to utilise video-conferencing between Belgrove High School and partner schools in France, Germany and Spain to support MFL teaching and learning. In practice, the video-conferencing had been sustained beyond the timescale originally envisaged, and remains an important means of improving students' conversational skills.

---

[4] See http://www.ocr.org.uk/.

CHAPTER 3: INNOVATIVE PEDAGOGY USING ICT

The case studies outlined in the previous chapter provide some examples of how ICT can help to change the nature of the interactions within primary and secondary school classrooms. This chapter highlights the themes and approaches that were evident across the six case studies and identifies points that teachers may consider before implementing any innovative practices in their own classrooms.

The cases featured can be divided into two main categories:

Category 1

1. Innovations which promote the involvement of others outside the physical classroom:
   - the epals project arranged with Ericsson by the BITC coordinator
   - the sections of Challenge 2000 that suggested pupils 'contact an expert for information'
   - the video-conferencing with students in France

Category 2

2. Innovations which change interactions within the classroom:
   - electronic communication between teacher and pupils
   - using a database to monitor and set targets for student performance
   - the computer as teacher in the on-line GNVQ course.

Of course, these two main categories are not mutually exclusive, for example Challenge 2000 work changed the interactions in the classroom from predominantly teacher:pupil to pupil:pupil, working in groups of four to seven. However, this chapter will consider some of the main features of the cases within the above categories.

A crucial point to emphasise is that none of the above cases required cutting-edge technology: the ICT employed in each practice (using the Internet, email, databases and video-conferencing facilities) had been widely available for several years. With the rapid pace of technological developments, it can sometimes appear that schools have to make substantial investments in new hardware and software in order to stimulate and challenge students. The introduction of these new resources often brings an associated demand for further training for teachers and classroom assistants, which can delay the effective implementation of new resources. In contrast, the SITES research deliberately set out to focus on innovative pedagogical practices rather than innovative technology. This means that the practices studied within the case-study schools could be adopted by greater numbers of teachers in other schools, as in most cases the ICT resources required to implement the innovation would be available in their school. Two of the innovations (Challenge 2000 and the on-line GNVQ) are already accessible by large numbers of students using the Internet.

3.1 Innovations which promote the involvement of others outside the physical classroom

The contribution that outside experts can make to students' learning was acknowledged from the inception of the NGfL, which provided an infrastructure linking schools, colleges, universities, museums, art galleries and other institutions connected with education and lifelong learning. Increasingly, at all levels of education, teachers are setting assignments for students which require them to search for information using the Internet. In some cases the required information can be extracted immediately from relevant Web sites, whereas in other instances students need to engage in dialogue with an expert, possibly by email.

The Challenge 2000 learning resource was deliberately designed to include activities which encouraged the students to contact an expert for specialist information: we observed a group of pupils deciding whom they should contact to obtain a translation of a short piece of text in Arabic, and one of the challenge developers reported that pupils had sent emails to an explorer on an expedition climbing the Himalayas. In total the explorer had received more than 100 emails from pupils working on the challenge and he had sent different individual replies to all of them, to provide assistance with their work.

In the case of the video-conferencing project, the outside experts were not adults with specialist skills, but students of a similar age in another country: during the video-conferencing sessions the students in England and in France spent some time speaking in their native language, and some time practising their conversational skills in the language they were learning. The subtleties of idioms and colloquial language were experienced in real contexts with native speakers. At the same time, the native English-speaking students were the experts to whom the French students were looking for examples of contemporary phrases and expressions.

The epals project at Woodford Junior School was intended to improve the literacy skills of particular pupils by encouraging them to communicate with an epal by email. One of the main aims in setting up the project was to put the pupils in touch with someone outside their immediate family, and importantly, someone who was in employment and could therefore provide information about the world of work, and help to raise pupils' aspirations. This was especially important because the school was situated in an area of social deprivation where very few people were employed and many had negative attitudes towards school and education. The contact with the epals at the Ericsson factory put the pupils in touch with adults (other than their own teachers) who were aware that employers looked for qualifications, individuals who could provide the encouragement to work hard at school that may have been lacking in the pupils' home environments. In addition, by using email as the method of communication rather than face-to-face contact, the pupils were gaining practical experience of a communication tool widely used in the contemporary workplace.

Although these three innovative practices are all very different, there are certain elements or themes that are common to all three.

♦ Firstly, in each case the others outside the students' classrooms were not involved in direct teaching: some schools have set up video-conferencing links so that one teacher can lead a lesson, involving pupils from different sites in a virtual classroom. In contrast, the practices described above led to the students interacting with individuals other than teachers as part of their learning activities. Their involvement provided new opportunities for the students concerned to communicate with someone other than individuals within their own family and school environments. In addition to developing students' communication skills, the activities also provided opportunities for them to develop their social skills.

♦ Secondly, each of the activities had some structure which guided the interactions with the individuals outside the classroom: these guidelines were either imposed from the outset (for example, the specific information that pupils working on Challenge 2000 were trying to find out, and the list of ten questions provided as a prompt for each of the video-conferencing sessions) or were subsequently introduced, as in the case of the epals project. In this instance, the participants on both sides were initially directed in general terms to find out about their partner. As the early exchanges were rather stilted in a number of cases, with some of the pupils failing to respond to the questions posed by the Ericsson employees, the coordinators at the school and at Ericsson each introduced activities to guide future communications. At the school, the teachers organised lessons focusing on how to write a letter, and the sort of questions you could direct to someone else, and from the Ericsson side, pupils were presented with a mini project to find out information about the company, which again helped them to focus on the sorts of question they needed to ask in order to find out the necessary information.

♦ Thirdly, there had to be an awareness of the ICT requirements both inside and outside the classroom. The head of the modern foreign languages department (MFL) who organised the video-conferencing sessions visited the partner school in order to set up the equipment and demonstrate how to use it. Inevitably, there were occasions when the sessions did not run smoothly and there were problems with the visual and/or the audio link. To enable the students involved in the sessions to cope with these situations, the MFL teacher had prepared a sheet listing typical problems, but also allowing space for students to specify another problem, which could be faxed to the partner school to alert them to the problem. Preliminary liaison between Woodford Junior School and the Ericsson company confirmed that both had access to Microsoft Word and email so that they could implement the epals project. However, some problems arose when partners attached files (for example, pupils showing examples of creative artwork) to their email messages which their partner could not open because they did not have the same software installed. In addition, when the project started the school had only one Internet connection (located in the school office): this caused some problems when all 25 pupils wanted to send their emails at the same time. These problems were resolved by encouraging the pupils to compose and send their email messages at home as well as by directing some of the email communication through the home email accounts of the teachers involved in the project. During one of our observations of Challenge 2000 work, one pupil left the class to phone an outside expert and returned some minutes later reporting that he had been asked to fax his request for information: these activities increased pupils' awareness of the range of technologies they could use.

♦ Fourthly, all three projects provide examples of how ICT can be used to counteract social and/or cultural isolation in a time- and cost-effective way. Both the video-conferencing and the Challenge 2000 activities provided opportunities for students to find out more about other cultures, by direct contact and by research covering a range of subjects including locations, individuals and religions. The epals project extended the social contact of pupils who came from families who were predominantly unemployed, and who tended to be socially isolated, rarely interacting with others outside their own housing estate. The communication with their epals therefore provided the pupils with information about alternative lifestyles, including work-related information that was unavailable in their own home environments and was intended to help to raise the pupils' own aspirations.

♦ Finally, pupils had to start to develop an awareness of, or empathy with, other people's points of view and commitments. In the case of the epals project, pupils had to learn that their partner might not be able to respond immediately to the email they had sent: for example, they may have been very busy with the work they were doing, in a meeting, or out of the office on a training course or on sick leave. This also applied to the children working on Challenge 2000; in addition, when they wanted to contact an expert for information, they had to provide background information in order to set their inquiry in an appropriate context. The video-conferencing sessions had to be scheduled at times that allowed for the different hours of the school day as well as the scheduling of different subjects within the timetable.

The students involved in these three practices were enthusiastic and motivated about the opportunities that the activities gave them to interact with others. At the same time, students involved in the epals project and in the video-conferencing sessions admitted that they had felt a little nervous or unsure of themselves in the initial exchanges. Each project utilised a different strategy to help overcome initial shyness: a few weeks after beginning the epals project, the pupils involved had visited the Ericsson factory to meet their epals face to face, and the video-conferencing was organised in small groups of two or three students, so that each one felt supported by one or more friends. The same groups of English and French students participated in the video-conferencing sessions at particular times each week, so that they all became more relaxed as they grew to know their partners. Similarly, the epals project maintained the same pairs of pupils and employees for the duration of the project, so that over time each became more knowledgeable about the other, and at ease.

3.2   Innovations which changed interactions within the classroom

Traditionally, the majority of lessons have been directed by the class teacher, who may utilise different approaches to organisation for particular activities. The SITES case studies demonstrate how ICT can offer opportunities to change the interactions within the classroom, changing the type of interactions between teacher and students, allowing students more direct interactions with resources to support learning and increasing the number of interactions between students themselves. The ICT adviser for one of the case-study schools summarised this shift in emphasis by saying: *'We're moving from teaching people everything to teaching people where they can find things out.'*

At Windmill Primary School, a class of 46 Year 6 pupils each had their own desktop PC which they could use all day every day. There was a high level of electronic communication in different ways:

Electronic
communication

- ♦   teacher to pupils
- ♦   pupils to teacher
- ♦   pupils to pupils
- ♦   pupils using the Internet: search engines and Web sites.

The pupils themselves noted that they could collaborate with other members of the class as part of a group without needing to sit together in a group: they could exchange ideas effectively using email or the MSN instant messaging service. All teachers and pupils within the school had their own email addresses, and pupils were actively encouraged to contact other people using the school network, but outside their own classroom, for specialist information. For example, the Year 6 teacher (who was also the ICT coordinator) reported that he frequently received emails from pupils throughout the school concerning problems with computer printers; pupils reported that they contacted a teacher in another class who was the science specialist. In this way, pupils throughout the school could seek specialist advice and information from teachers other than their own class teacher. As all children had access to the Internet all day, they became accustomed to seeking information on the World Wide Web, rather than asking their teacher or one of the classroom assistants.

At Highgrove High School, the staff had developed their own computer database for monitoring student achievement and setting targets. As a school with almost 2000 students on roll, Heads of Year commented that it was very difficult to monitor individual students' progress in all subjects across the curriculum before they had started using their own ICT-based system. Within the lower school, the database was predominantly used for recording student achievement in formal tests (such as tests at the end of Key Stages 2 and 3, and NFER Cognitive Abilities Tests administered in Years 7 and 9) and the grades attained in different modules of each subject. Within the upper school the results from the YELLIS and ALIS predictive tests taken by students in Years 10 and 12 supplemented the achievement data already recorded for each individual student. Together with the information about student performance in different subjects amassed over the students' secondary school careers, the predictive data formed the basis of a discussion with each student to discuss their target grades in the formal GCSE examinations at 16+ or the A-level examinations at 18+ as appropriate. Thus, the interactions between teachers and students were more focused on the students' potential achievements as a result of having the student tracking database.

The two-year on-line GNVQ course at Coleridge College led to an intermediate level award, which was equivalent to four GCSE passes at grades A*–C. In this case, each session was focused on individual work in response to the course assignments and assessment requirements provided by the on-line resource materials, rather than teacher-directed activities: students interacted predominantly with their computer, and only occasionally with their peers or with the teacher supervising the session.

As with the innovations which promoted the involvement of others outside the physical classroom, the three practices outlined above are all very different, but again there are some common themes relating to all three.

♦   Firstly, in all three cases students experienced greater independence and responsibility for their own work and progress. At Windmill Primary School, the pupils had a short list of assignments that they had to work on at any one time, but they had considerable freedom to choose which one they wanted to work on at a particular time. Students at Coleridge College were able to access their on-line course during the formal after-school sessions, during scheduled homework sessions at school, and at home either via the Internet or by using a CD-ROM containing all the materials for that term. Consequently, students could choose when and where to do the additional one hour of unsupervised work per week that was a course requirement. Students at Highgrove High School were encouraged to take responsibility for the grades they received in all their assessed work, and were aware that if their performance deteriorated their teachers would very quickly identify their lower grades and would meet with them to discuss the cause of the problem and ways in which they could improve their attainment again.

♦ Secondly, all three practices involved students in working towards targets and/or deadlines for the submission of work, a practice that had changed the nature of teacher–student interaction. At Windmill Primary School, the Year 6 teacher set specific pieces of work to be completed by the pupils over a period of up to two weeks; he issued reminders of ongoing tasks by email to the whole class using a distribution list, and could prompt selected pupils about specific activities in individual email messages. The Year 10 students at Coleridge College had been introduced to the course format by the teachers running the different sessions, but subsequently there had been minimal input from the teachers: typically, they moved around the class during each session providing assistance when required. As the deadline for the submission of an assignment approached, the teachers reminded students of the deadline. Whilst the targets at Windmill and Coleridge involved specific deadlines for particular pieces of work, the targets at Highgrove were concerned with student achievement as expressed in grades to be attained for specific subjects. In addition, the target-setting and review process was ongoing for all subjects throughout each student's career at Highgrove, so that past performance continually contributed to future targets. Typically, the setting of target grades for students to aim for in their GCSE and A-level examinations was a process negotiated between subject teachers and individual students drawing on the information stored in the student-tracking database about past performance.

♦ Finally, there was evidence that the innovations fostered ongoing reflection about their work. For the pupils at Windmill Primary School, the move to the majority of their work being produced using a PC rather than by using pen and paper methods had resulted in a new approach to work: producing a first draft, submitting it to the teacher for comments and review, then revising and refining their work. Frequently this process was achieved using ICT tools, for example the teacher returning a draft piece of work with particular sections highlighted, or with comments and amendments suggested using the 'track changes' facility in Word. Similarly, students taking the on-line GNVQ course produced first drafts of work, and compared them with those of other students, so that they could see the approaches adopted by their peers. They were also able to review their own work alongside the assessment criteria for the assignments (available on-line) and consider whether or not their work met the standards required. At Highgrove, the evidence of students' past performance was used by teachers to encourage the students to review their strengths and weaknesses, and to discuss ways in which they could improve their performance (for example, by receiving specific support in particular areas).

3.3   Other impacts on students

Some of the positive impacts that the innovations have had on the students involved have been in the sections above.   Comments from some of those who observed the impact on students indicated additional benefits:

♦   Parents in different schools reported that their children showed them how to carry out particular tasks using different software packages and/or the Internet, and some mentioned it as an opportunity for strengthening their relationship with their children: *'I don't know about PCs, but she shows me how to do things and it's a bonding process'*; *'[It's a chance] for us to learn, yes. Some people are interested and some aren't... I'm up on it and interested. He likes the thought that he knows more than we do about technology... He helps me a lot. He did some business cards and the letters for a job I was doing.'*

♦   One ICT adviser suggested that the students' personal presentation skills had been enhanced as a result of taking part in the video-conferencing sessions: *'It's broader than just the language skills – personal presentation and social skills... a lot of children don't have presentation skills and I think that if we're in an employment era where first contacts mean a lot, presentation is very important and it is a spin off from video-conferencing.'*

♦   The development of self-directed study skills was seen as useful preparation for higher education: *'...research* [using the Internet] *has to be relevant and succinct – prepares them for university;'* *'[the on-line GNVQ course] makes students more autonomous, in charge of their own learning and makes them have to take responsibility for their own learning which is useful preparation for university.'* In fact, the increased independence and motivation for self-directed study developed by students involved in the innovative practices was valuable preparation for lifelong learning.

♦   Especially within the primary schools, the innovations provided opportunities for less able pupils to participate equally in activities, and to have their own achievements and skills celebrated by their peers. One headteacher remarked: *'ICT is a leveller and all children can learn to use ICT in order to learn what they want from it. Those who are not high performers can be when using ICT'*; another explained that ICT *'...has also helped pupils with educational and behavioural disorders: for the first time in their careers they have felt success. If they want to participate, they can, there's no exclusion. They have not benefited more than others, but have been given the opportunity to be successful.'*

Some negative impacts on students were also evident: at Windmill Primary School, some pupils were voluntarily spending time outside lessons (before school, during morning and lunch breaks) working on their computer – in some cases this may have reduced pupils' opportunities for physical activities outside the classroom; similarly, students participating in the video-conferencing sessions had to give up part of their lunch break; and students who volunteered for the on-line GNVQ course had an increased workload in Years 10 and 11. Some parents indicated that although their children were keen to spend time using a computer at home in the evening, they felt it was important to encourage other activities as well.

3.4   Implications for schools

Apart from skills in using the ICT involved in these innovative practices, the teachers concerned had to be willing to change their existing practices: in several of the cases students became more independent and supported each other; students developed new communication and social skills; and students improved their self-directed study skills. Clearly, teachers had to accept changes in their role and in the interactions they had with students. In addition, teachers had to support their students as their roles changed too. At the same time, teachers had to monitor the implementation of the activities they introduced, and identify possible solutions to any problems that arose. The introduction of innovative practices therefore placed additional demands on teachers, not only in relation to the organisation of the activities, but also in managing the changing interactions within and outside the classroom. Despite the time and effort required to manage these changes, the teachers involved in the SITES case studies all agreed that the outcomes justified the effort, and were positive about sustaining the initiatives that they had been involved in.

A common thread emerging from the different cases was a willingness (at both senior management and class-teacher level) to try new approaches, with an awareness that some would not succeed, but acknowledging that only stagnation results from reluctance to try new practices. One headteacher reported '*We have stopped doing things that haven't worked in the past. We're getting somewhere – it* [video-conferencing] *has an impact*'. Another headteacher explained:

> *I heard a speech about taking the next step, having the confidence to take the next step and in this school I want everyone to have the confidence to do that for themselves – the teachers, everyone. Part of the evolving culture is that everyone has the confidence to take a risk and fail. If you don't, you only achieve a certain level because you never take what you can from the learning opportunity.*

For the teachers involved in the SITES case studies therefore, the innovative activities that they were involved in all took place within the context of a school environment where there was a culture of exploring new approaches. In each case, the school and/or the teachers concerned had had previous involvement in educational innovations, some of which had involved ICT. The prevailing culture within the schools was one of collaboration and mutual support: in all cases the headteachers were enthusiastic about, and in some instances actively involved in, the innovations. This undoubtedly helped to smooth a number of the administrative difficulties that were encountered in setting up several of the innovative practices.

Importantly, key features of the management style within the case-study schools were:

- A clear, shared vision of school goals, which was embodied in both the practices and plans for future development within the school. For example, staff at Woodford Junior School referred to their aim of increasing the ICT skills of the local community, as well as those of their pupils, and encouraging pupils to take the school laptops home was one of a number of ways in which the school set out to increase access to ICT for the wider community.

- A willingness to take managed risks, and to find creative ways of meeting their needs. One example of this was the case of Windmill Primary School, which had a policy of providing appropriate resources to allow all pupils to achieve their potential. The headteacher and staff agreed that, in accordance with this policy, an effective way of enabling ICT to enhance pupils' learning would be to provide one PC per child in the final year of primary education (Year 6). The headteacher explained the two main strategies he had used to fund the acquisition of the additional machines from the school budget:

    Firstly, it depends on the management set-up of the money within the school. We don't keep small amounts of money, just one budget overall. . . Small amounts for each department [area of the curriculum] *won't buy anything, but by using the money as a whole, more benefit can be found for all departments. Secondly, we lease everything, which gives us the opportunity to have the machines now, within budget.*

- Entrepreneurial skills in approaching a variety of organisations for support and/or resources that would impact on the school. The headteacher at Belgrove High School had established effective links with a range of organisations including: the BBC, Granada Learning, the Open University, the European Union, the then Department for Education and Employment, IBM, and ICL. As a result of these links, the school had benefited in a number of ways, including receiving funding and equipment, and establishing new courses for students. In this school, and others, a proactive approach seemed to pay dividends.

Finally, some points that other schools may want to consider before adopting any innovative practices involving ICT include:

Points for consideration

1. Are the aims clear and shared by all those involved?

2. Who (teachers/students/others) will be involved – will interested individuals be able to volunteer, or will the practice focus on certain target groups?

3. What permission and/or checks should be obtained/carried out before introducing the practice?

4. When, where and how frequently will the activity take place?

5. What skills are required in order to participate? Is specific training for teachers and/or students necessary?

6. What resources are required, in the school and elsewhere (for example, at home, or in other locations)?

7. How does the activity fit in with other school/LEA/national practices and priorities?

8. Will the activity have a finite duration (e.g. several weeks/months/ a year) or will it be ongoing?

9. What outcomes are required, who will evaluate them and how?

10. Is it practical to introduce the innovation as a small-scale trial, so that any difficulties can be resolved before extending the practice?

The innovative practices in the six case study schools were not implemented without a number of problems, but where difficulties arose, those involved worked to find solutions, some of which are described in the next chapter. There were positive impacts on the students who participated in the innovative practices in terms of motivation, confidence, skills, and achievement, as well as suggestions of long-term benefits too, perhaps influencing students' choices for higher education and employment.

The clear message from these case studies concerns not the importance of ICT in its own right, but the benefits to be gained when confident teachers are willing to explore new opportunities for changing their classroom practices by utilising ICT.

The final chapter presents more details of the six innovations studied.

CHAPTER 4: THE SITES CASE STUDIES IN ENGLAND

This chapter provides detailed information about the six case studies (three primary and three secondary) carried out in schools in England as part of SITES. Within each case, the text focuses on the curriculum being implemented, the technology used and the impact on both teachers and students. References to the 'innovation teacher' within each case refer to the teacher(s) of the class using the innovative approach.

4.1 Case Study – Primary 1

Windmill Primary School – All-day access to their own PC for each pupil in Year 6

4.1.1 Curriculum content, goals and assessment

The school was well-equipped with ICT resources: there were 100 computers within the school, with half of these located in the main Year 6 teaching area. Other year groups had computer:pupil ratios of between 1:14 and 1:4. There was general agreement that the use of computers throughout the school had not changed curriculum content and goals: rather, the computers were regarded as a tool to support teaching and learning across the curriculum. This was most evident in Year 6, where all 46 pupils had access to their own desktop PC all day, every day (see photo 1). The innovation teacher commented:

> *The curriculum has remained the same and so has my teaching style and rapport with the children ... The advantage is that at all stages of that work, research, planning, collecting data, presentation, Web site development, etc. [ICT] enables the children to get on with their work and produce a high- quality product without waiting for a PC. The concept of one each has made a big difference. ... What has changed is the methodology and the fact that more is possible.*

Year 6 pupils were set assignments, which they usually took one to two weeks to complete. They could choose their own approach to the assignment: either using ICT (with more than 15 programs available in addition to Internet access) or more traditional methods of working. The innovation teacher explained that the assignments allowed pupils to develop the work at their own level:

> *The majority of the activities are open-ended, matched with work relevant to certain children. ... We don't like closed work where they do it and it is marked. We use more creative work. I set the structure and they will create something more original and personal – more of the original work. We do use the Internet and intranet to support the activities which I will make available for them either via the intranet or email.*

One of the two Learning Support Assistants (LSAs) working in Year 6 commented, *'They extend the things they're asked to do according to their interests – take the tasks much further than expected in other classes'*.

Files could be electronically exchanged between pupils and teacher, allowing the teacher to comment on work in progress and suggest amendments where appropriate. Pupils noted how they could improve their work simply by editing selected parts:

> Pupil 2: *We have a first go and* [the teacher] *points out what we have to change – he goes through everyone's work. He sends it back with tracking* [track changes in Word documents] *or highlighting.*

> Pupil 3: *It's different – we get a chance to change it without starting all over again.*

> Pupil 4: *We can just alter the spelling mistakes.*

The whole school used a web-based assessment procedure (*The Educator*[5]): this had been trialled during the 1998–99 school year and fully implemented since the 1999–00 school year. *The Educator* allowed teachers to record the pupils' performance against the National Curriculum requirements. The innovation teacher assessed pupils in English, mathematics and science once or twice each term, and for some pupils making slower progress, twice a year[6].

Both the innovation teacher and the headteacher stressed the importance of effective assessment, as it helped teachers to plan the next activities for pupils at an appropriate level. The headteacher commented, *'The planning is directly linked to the assessment'*, and the innovation teacher explained that this was part of the whole-school approach:

> *... you need good assessment, need to plan for every child, create activities that meet that plan and provide extension, motivation and purpose for that child. The assessment then forms a critical part of the system. We use ICT to make the assessments and to track the progress.* [What happens in my class is] *not different to other teachers in the school...*

4.1.2 Kinds of technology and ways they are used

Within Year 6 there were 50 desktop PCs linked as part of the whole school network, plus two laptops. This allowed one PC per pupil plus a few spares in the event of any problems. The two LSAs who worked full-time in the class were able to use any of the machines not being used by the children.

---

[5] See www.the-educator.co.uk .
[6] Pupils are typically expected to take two years to progress from one level of National Curriculum achievement to the next (e.g. two years to progress from level three to level four). The Educator helps to break down the progress into four smaller stages so that teachers can monitor pupils' progress more accurately.

Each pupil's machine had the following installed:

Software

Corel Xara2	Microsoft Publisher 2000
Adobe Photoshop	Microsoft Word 2000
CD-Roms	Microsoft Messenger
Internet Explorer 5	Netchess
Micro Logic	PinPoint
Microsoft Front Page	Primary Clip Art Browser
Microsoft Outlook 2000	Textease
Microsoft PowerPoint 2000	Windows Media Player

Each machine was equipped with speakers and headphones so that pupils could use multimedia resources (see photo 2). The teacher had two PCs on his desk, one of which was connected to the interactive whiteboard, and the other provided access to the range of applications available. The class had a data projector which could be used for whole-class demonstrations.

The innovation teacher explained how these resources had extended the ways in which he could communicate effectively with all pupils:

> I used a [conventional] whiteboard before, but now I can send that information to them, keep records, break down information for different groups of children. I use the projector to show examples of children's work, examples of what I want them to do. The communication angle has changed. I still talk to children, but now I can communicate with them through email, Web pages, they can send me work. I can go through their work remotely as well now. Microsoft Messenger gives them live communication and they can talk to me through the computer on a one-to-one basis.

The LSAs referred to the value of the files sent from the interactive whiteboard for all pupils, but especially those with special educational needs (SEN):

> A: Anything that goes up on the board can be recorded on anyone's PC rather than having to strain to look at the board. They can call up information from three weeks ago which would have been wiped off a board. Especially good for the SEN children in the class.
>
> B: They don't have to worry about copying things down.
>
> A: It increases self-confidence and they don't get worried.

Other ICT resources available in Year 6 included: a scanner, digital cameras, a digital video camera, laser printers, CD writers and zip drives. A music keyboard with a midi interface to a PC was also available, and the children had produced a CD of their own recordings. A planned development was to add an additional set of headphones to each pupil's PC with a boom for using voice recognition software (Dragon Naturally Speaking).

The children were able to search the Internet at any time to help them with their work, as well as using materials for their class placed on the intranet by their teacher. Internet access was screened using an appropriate filter provided by the hardware supplier to prevent pupils accessing undesirable material; pupils were aware that any attempts to view inappropriate material would result in removal of Internet access.

4.1.3 Teacher practices and outcomes

The innovation teacher used the technology available to him in almost all subject areas. He commented on how the curriculum remained the main focus rather than the machines, due to each pupil having their own desktop computer and becoming familiar with using the technology. He had had no formal ICT training, but as the headteacher said, '*The competency of each teacher is dependent on their personality, wanting to try something out, to make it work better.*'

The innovation teacher referred to the need to keep exploring new resources. He called it '*a never-ending journey*' and added that '*once you feel confident, it's not as difficult to try things out*'.

The innovative nature of the classroom environment did lead to some changes in teacher practice. The role of the teacher had altered in the areas of delivery, instruction, and assessment. For example, the class teacher often sent an email to the whole class at the start of the school day (see sample email in Appendix II). The teacher also used email to send additional information to higher or lower ability pupils in order to provide either extension or further assistance to an activity. We observed him using a data projector for a whole-class activity, demonstrating how to design a layout for a PinPoint questionnaire. Another impact of the technology on the teacher's role was in the use of an automated marking system for the daily mental arithmetic test, which returned details of correct and incorrect responses to pupils, as well as sending a copy to the class teacher's files.

The innovation had provided alternative methods of instruction by means of pupil task lists. Each child would add their own tasks to this list, enabling them to carry out the necessary work by the predetermined deadline. This meant that the teacher did not have to constantly remind the class of work to be done. One of the LSAs in the Year 6 class said that he thought '...[pupils'] *attitudes might have changed to what is work. They always communicated before, but they're now doing it in a different way.*'

The parents thought that the teacher's role had remained the same, regardless of the computers. One parent commented: '*It's no different. He still does the same sort of work, just with a different tool*'. The innovation teacher himself thought that his approach to teaching had remained the same: '*I use the technology as part of my teaching. ICT is one aspect of what I use.*'

The impact of the innovation on the teacher–pupil interaction in the class was largely due to the pupils having more responsibility for their own learning and task management. We observed both the teacher and the LSAs assisting pupils on a one-to-one basis, advising pupils on ways in which they could draft, improve and refine their work. However, we also noticed that there were fewer interactions between the teacher and pupils, due to pupils obtaining support and information from sources other than the adults in the classroom, such as the Internet, the intranet and other pupils.

4.1.4 Student practices and outcomes

We observed pupils using Microsoft Word to write stories and reports of a science experiment (dissolving sugar in water) (see photo 3 for an example of another science report); using CorelXara to produce a diagram of the equipment used in the same science experiment and to prepare a grid for a crossword puzzle; and using Microsoft Publisher to design a Valentine card. In each of these cases, the pupils could choose to use software or produce the work manually.

Twice each day all Year 6 pupils worked on the same activity at the same time:

- **the school day began with a short mental arithmetic test**: all children attempted the same test and received an automated email indicating their results (see photo 4);

- **afternoon school started with Starspell (multimedia) to practise spelling** – children worked for approximately 10 minutes at different levels according to their ability.

One of the LSAs described a typical pupil's day as follows:

Come in about half an hour before school starts, log on, check their emails, look through the task list they have to finish. They might design a birthday card for a family member, etc., during this half an hour which is still their own time. ... Then they get onto mental arithmetic every day – access through school intranet and class server – and any other work to finish off. Language – comprehension, a newspaper article, etc. Then break – some stay in to go on the Internet to find out about their hobbies, then maths. Lunch – stay in again and send emails, etc. Science, art, games, music and other various subjects in the afternoon. [They] Will stay back after school too, to make a CD [record their own music].

There was wide agreement amongst school staff, parents and pupils that individual access to a PC had benefited pupils in a number of ways:

Benefits

- **motivation**: pupils were more enthusiastic about school work;

- **presentation of work**: all pupils, irrespective of ability, were able to produce well presented, attractive work;

- **the inclusion of pupils with special educational needs (including behavioural disorders)**: *the headteacher commented, '... for the first time in their careers they have felt success. They can all go as far as they can go.* [There is] *No exclusion in opportunity';*

- **ability to work independently**: each pupil decides whether to use ICT or traditional methods for a particular task;

Benefits

♦ **ability to organise their work (i.e. prioritise)**: pupils have to maintain progress with existing assignments as well as responding to new tasks; they use Outlook to list tasks set/completed;

♦ **learning gains**: the headteacher stated, '*The evidence of children applying themselves is in the work*', and referred to high achievement in National Curriculum assessments[7] for pupils;

♦ **confidence and self-esteem**: pupils of all abilities worked confidently and purposefully, and were proud of the work they produced.

Comments from pupils indicated that although other teachers had also set extended tasks to be completed over several days, much more communication was done electronically in Year 6:

Pupil 1: *It's more through the PCs than it was before. It used to be books and the teacher at the front of the class.* [Now there is] *not as much talking at the board.*

Pupil 4: *He sends work back by email so we don't have to queue or worry about not hearing what to do.* [There is] *no way we can miss anything if an email is sent to you.*

ICT also supported communication and collaboration with others, for example using email or the real-time message service Microsoft Messenger to communicate with other members of a group without having to move places: '*...we can share ideas in groups, even in silence.*' Pupils (throughout the school) were also able to email other teachers with questions relating to their ongoing work, e.g. send questions about science to the science coordinator, and ICT questions (such as printing problems) to the ICT coordinator.

---

[7] National Curriculum assessments are mandatory for pupils in Years 2, 6 and 9 (ages seven, 11 and 14) in state schools. The results achieved by pupils in Years 6 and 9 are published in school performance tables. Data for the year 2000 show that the results achieved by Year 6 pupils at Windmill Primary School in the tests in English, mathematics and science were higher than the averages within the local education authority and England as a whole, and exceeded the government's targets for pupil performance for the year 2002.

4.2   Case Study – Primary 2

Woodford Junior School – Writing for a real purpose: communication by email between ten-year-olds and employees at a mobile phone factory

4.2.1   Curriculum content, goals and assessment

The epals scheme was primarily an approach to boost self-esteem, personal and social skills. It had been set up with the assistance of a regional coordinator for Business in the Community (BITC – a national organisation which encourages businesses to become involved in the activities of the local community), and linked a group of Year 5 pupils at Woodford Junior School with volunteers at the nearby Ericsson[8] mobile phone factory. Each pupil was allocated an epal at the factory to communicate with, sharing information about current work, family members, hobbies, etc. by email. The scheme was intended to develop pupils' literacy and ICT skills. A Year 6 teacher spoke of the benefits:

> ... it's a wonderful idea – the children are insular so this gives them an idea of outside life. The children's questions [to their epals] at the beginning were naïve – 'Are you rich?' 'Do you live in a big house?' It gave them a window on the world. Hopefully it gives them someone who will listen to them and who is interested in them – a sympathetic friend and someone to encourage them in their academic attainment.

One parent said that the epals scheme focused more on 'social skills than the curriculum'. The BITC coordinator remarked:

> The aim of the project was to give children the opportunity to develop vital IT and communication skills, and provide them with an inspiring insight into the world of work.

When it started in summer 2000, one of the two Year 5 teachers coordinated the pupils' involvement. The scheme had continued beyond the original one-term duration envisaged, and as the Year 5 epals coordinator had moved into Year 6, he continued to oversee the work.

There was no formal assessment of pupils' epals work by the school, but the BITC coordinator carried out analysis of the changes in pupils' skills as a result of their involvement in the epals project, based on pupils' self-ratings before and after the project (see section 4.2.4 below and Appendix III).

4.2.2   Kinds of technology and ways they are used

The pupils involved in the project needed a desktop or laptop computer with email, an email account, a modem and a phone point; the epals at Ericsson all

---

[8]   The coordinator of the scheme within the company authorised it to be identified by name.

needed access to similar equipment. The 25 laptops[9] used by the children in Year 5 all had Microsoft Office (including Outlook Express) and modems installed, and allowed each child involved in the project to have access to a machine for contacting their epal either from school or from home. In addition, some pupils had sent/received attachments with their emails (e.g. Word documents, clip-art and pictures they had scanned). The BITC coordinator commented that for future schemes the company's IT department should be involved to check the software available to both parties in the project to ensure that attachments could be opened: the issue of software incompatibility or different versions of the same software could be sources of difficulties.

Teachers and pupils reported occasional difficulties when some of the laptops were unavailable due to low battery power, being sent away for repair or machines having been stolen. The greatest problem that had to be overcome within the school was the limited Internet access: although all the laptops were fitted with modems, there was only one phone line in the school '... *under the desk in the school office*', and as a result the children were encouraged to send their emails from home wherever possible. Again, teachers and pupils mentioned this as being a problem, and the teachers suggested that the project would have run more smoothly if there had been additional phone lines either in the classrooms or in the ICT suite.

The Ericsson factory was located about 30 miles away from the school, so email was a time- and cost-effective way of maintaining communication between the epals. The ICT coordinator stated:

> *It's providing a link that wouldn't be there any other way... Technology is providing an impetus, drive and enthusiasm as well as making the link and communication easier. We've tried before to set up a similar programme without ICT, where we tried to link up with another school, but it wasn't as effective.*

The BITC coordinator commented, '*The amount of time employees can take off work is limited, but 20 minutes per week means employees can do this without leaving their desk and it is manageable for them.*'

4.2.3   Teacher practices and outcomes

Teachers carried out four main activities in connection with the innovation:

Main activities

♦   identifying pupils who would benefit from taking part in the epals project, and passing on background information about these pupils to Ericsson

♦   ensuring that pupils taking part had the necessary skills to communicate by email

♦   providing opportunities during the school day for pupils to access and send emails

♦   monitoring the outgoing and incoming emails.

---

[9]   The school had acquired these laptops when it piloted the Microsoft Anytime Anywhere Learning scheme in 1998. The laptops were shared across the two Year 5 classes and stayed with the pupils when they moved into Year 6; they were used both at school and at home. Each machine was shared between two or three named pupils and these pupils negotiated between themselves when they wanted to take the laptop home to use.

The two teachers who were involved in the project had to be competent in using email (Microsoft Outlook Express). They showed the pupils how to use email, and provided guidance about the sort of information they could put in their emails:

> *To begin with we let them write what they wanted to, but we found that the lower ability ones needed more help so we showed them some guided writing. On overheads we showed them the kind of stuff to talk about and we did a mind map. We taught this in the literacy class for epals, and for those not on the scheme it taught them how to write a letter.*

Both the Year 5 teachers stated that the approach they had adopted for organising classroom activities related to epals was similar to the way they worked generally: for some lessons one teacher would take a mixed group of children from across the two classes for a particular activity, and the other teacher would organise a different activity for the other children.

> *In their lessons they would learn how to set up and send emails and that would take an afternoon, then they were encouraged to do the same from home ... Last term we were doing it during lesson times and providing them with opportunities to extend this at home. Typically one session a week or every other – two hours minimum a fortnight over six to eight weeks.*

Both Year 5 teachers reported that by monitoring the content of the emails that pupils were sending to their epals, they gained additional insights into what the children liked and disliked:

> *It's been interesting to witness what motivates the students. We give them suggestions but they are free to write what they want to, so it gives us an insight into the mind of the child that we wouldn't have had if it wasn't for this. They are guarded when they talk to teachers, but are open when they talk to the epals.*

The epals project fitted in with the two Year 5 teachers' visions of teaching and learning, in which learning should be fun, and pupils should have regular opportunities to develop their confidence as computer users.

4.2.4 Student practices and outcomes

The two Year 5 teachers identified 25 pupils[10] across the year group whom they thought would benefit from having adults to communicate with. Various criteria for selecting children were mentioned, including *'no male figure in the home'*, or other home circumstances:

> *One factor we looked at was whether the children get much attention at home, and we particularly picked children that we were worried about – those who need more attention because they were part of a large family or living with grandparents...*

---

[10] The epals scheme was set up as a one-term (summer term) project for 25 Year 5 children; following positive feedback at the end of the first term, it was agreed to continue the project for a second term (autumn term) when the children had entered Year 6. Not all Ericsson epals wanted to continue beyond the planned duration, so only ten children continued for the second term.

and:

> *The children were chosen to give them someone interested in them and the motivation for writing. We selected de-motivated children because some have PCs at home and are already into IT so we wouldn't choose them.*

Each pupil was linked to one employee (epal) at the Ericsson company: they exchanged emails on a regular basis, which gave the pupils an opportunity to practise their communication and ICT skills. The project was unusual because ten-year-old pupils rarely communicate over an extended period with adults other than teachers and their own family and seldom use email as their main means of communication with another person. This was acknowledged by the pupils: *'It was strange at first because we didn't know the people and what they are like. It was better after three or four emails'*; and, *'It was good to meet them'* [on the trip to the Ericsson factory[11]].

Pupils usually drafted their emails in Outlook Express on their laptop, but occasional problems (e.g. using a different machine because their own had been sent off for repair) meant they sometimes wrote them using Word (see photos 5 and 6), then sent the file as an attachment to an email.

Both the Year 5 teachers and the headteacher felt that the children were more proficient using Word than Outlook Express: *'Word is more child-friendly because with Outlook Express you have to have quite a few things exactly right for it to work'*, *'Pupils find Outlook quite difficult to use.'*

This presented difficulties for some children who wanted to send emails from home:

> *The brighter children have done well with it* [Outlook Express], *but those with poor memory skills haven't because by the time they got home they couldn't remember what to do* [how to send an email].

Teachers noted that the children involved in the epals project developed improved attitudes to school work, better communications skills, increased motivation and raised awareness of the world of work. One teacher commented:

> *I noticed with a couple of girls their mentor was asking them about their geography topic and asking them questions, and they used it* [looked for information on the Internet] *which they wouldn't have bothered to look for in a book.*

The BITC coordinator remarked:

> *...one told his epal that he likes making moving things, so that epal helped the pupil, found him information and suggested ideas for how to make it* [the model] *better.*

---

[11] The children involved in the epals project went on a visit to the Ericsson factory partway through the first term. It provided an opportunity for many (but not all) of the children to meet their epals for the first time.

Because this was a new project, the BITC coordinator was keen to evaluate the impact it had had on the pupils, so she interviewed them individually and asked them to rate their own levels in a range of eight areas of knowledge, skills and attitudes[12] before and after taking part in the project. Her analysis showed that after taking part in the epals project, pupils were more motivated about school work, and had improved their ICT, literacy and social skills. (The results of the BITC evaluation are presented in Appendix III.)

There was general agreement that a major benefit of the epals project was the way it had helped to raise children's aspirations and awareness of lifelong learning, which is important in an area of social deprivation where education is not valued and unemployment is widespread.

The BITC coordinator commented:

> *Most* [of these] *children have limited aspirations and experiences, so conversations with someone from the world of work will inspire the children and broaden their horizons. It's about making them connect success in adult life to work at school.*

One of the teachers stated:

> *A good thing is the link with the world of work. There are fairly low expectations of employment on the estate, people generally don't see the need for qualifications, but* [the link with] *Ericsson has made a difference and had an effect on their thinking. For example,* [during the visit to the factory] *one child asked, 'Can I work here?' and the mentor replied, 'Only if you work hard and get qualified.'*

Once the project had been set up and the pupils were competent in sending their own emails, they were encouraged to communicate with their epals by using their laptops at home. This also provided opportunities for their parents/ guardians to see the sort of communications that were taking place.

---

[12] The eight areas were:
- computer skills
- email ability
- Internet ability
- confidence in talking to people not known
- writing ability
- knowledge about work
- ambitions for the future
- keenness to come to school.

4.3   Case Study – Primary 3

Moorcroft Primary School – Challenge 2000: an Internet-based resource for stimulating cooperative group work including cross-curricular research, problem-solving and cultural awareness

4.3.1   Curriculum content, goals and assessment

Challenge 2000 was a cross-curricular resource set in the context of a round-the-world balloon trip, presenting pupils with monthly challenges, divided into stages, which had to be achieved to continue the journey. The problems and investigations posed within each month's questions covered a wide range of subjects, as the following examples show:

♦ **English/language/literacy**: reading the content of the Web pages and other sources of information, and communicating with others in a variety of ways;

♦ **mathematics**: using codes involving numbers, calculating equivalent sums of money in different currencies;

♦ **geography**: locating different countries/cities/sea masses on maps; compass directions;

♦ **history**: researching famous people and events in different cultures;

♦ **music**: using musical notation, recording a version of a country's national anthem;

♦ **design technology**: constructing a model hot air balloon;

♦ **ICT**: carrying out Internet searches, using email, a digital camera, and presentation software.

The material was presented as a monthly challenge spread over 6–10 multimedia Web pages (see Appendix IV for extracts from one month's challenge); the pages posed questions to which the pupils had to find answers, and problems to solve. There were three main elements to each month's material:

Main elements

1. cross-curricular problems and investigations which led to different cities/countries;

2. preparation of a 'travelogue' presenting information about the culture of each place where the balloon landed;

3. a practical task to encourage creativity.

The material had been developed to allow a range of different learning strategies and approaches to problem-solving, so that pupils could choose their preferred approaches.

These materials:

- ♦ provided visual, auditory and kinaesthetic activities
- ♦ included activities that required logical thought
- ♦ presented opportunities to develop and demonstrate understanding
- ♦ encouraged original thinking and imaginative solutions to problems
- ♦ promoted effective organisation of effort within teams or groups.

Group or team work was actively promoted by the materials: there were too many questions for any one child to answer within the intended time, and the problems were structured to encourage pupils to share their ideas about how to solve them. When a group had completed all the questions/problems for one month's stage of the journey, their balloon progressed to the next location. Each group placed an outline of their own balloon on a large map of the world to record their current position (see photo 7).

Within Moorcroft, all Year 6 pupils worked on Challenge 2000 during class time for approximately one hour each week. The 44 children were grouped into teams of between four and seven pupils. Typically, half the class withdrew from the Year 6 classroom for Challenge 2000 – three groups worked in the studio (ten computers – see photo 8), and one group worked in the upper school ICT cluster (eight machines). One of the two Year 6 teachers (the innovation teacher) supervised pupils in the studio, those in the upper school cluster were not directly supervised by a Year 6 teacher, but the two Year 4 teachers were nearby. Pupils could also work on Challenge 2000 during after-school 'club' sessions, usually held 3–4pm Tuesday–Friday each week; some Year 5 pupils also attended the after-school club and formed a group on their own. In observations of sessions we saw that teams divided into smaller working groups (often pairs and individuals) to work on different aspects of the challenge; in some instances, part of the group worked on the fourth challenge while others started on the fifth challenge.

The cross-curricular format was in accordance with Moorcroft Primary School's preference for using a thematic approach to learning, but was considerably different from the National Curriculum structure, which presents programmes of study for particular subjects, together with an associated assessment framework.

Because Challenge 2000 was an extended activity (September 2000 to June 2001), pupils were not able to check their answers until the end of the project. However, children's work on Challenge 2000 provided opportunities for the innovation teacher to assess pupils' skills, predominantly their ICT skills, but also others, such as their personal and social skills (for example, their ability to work effectively as part of a team), and literacy (for example, their communication skills in constructing emails). She commented:

> *When they began we knew that their* [ICT] *knowledge was very high, but gaps showed and we fill in those... They're not in a class structure and the group dynamics are incredible... I've seen aspects of development that I've not seen in other subjects. They construct emails, letters, presentations which all helps literacy and social skills...*

4.3.2 Kinds of technology and ways they are used

Challenge 2000 was accessed from the LEA Grid for Learning: the minimum resources required were therefore one or more computers with Internet access. Because the Challenge 2000 materials were available via the Internet, they could be used by any institution worldwide. Pupils could use a wide range of ICT resources when responding to the questions posed in the challenge, such as:

ICT resources

- ♦ **software** – Word, PowerPoint, Textease, Front Page, Publisher, Encarta, Eyewitness World Atlas (see photo 9)

- ♦ **peripherals** – digital camera, microphones, headphones, scanner

- ♦ **Internet resources** – Web sites and different search engines: we saw pupils using Yahoo, Ask Jeeves, Lycos, Alta Vista, Google and Yell

- ♦ **communication devices** – telephones, mobile phones and faxes.

There were 18 PCs altogether available for pupils to use outside the main classroom (ten in the studio and eight in the upper school cluster), so pupils could easily work either individually, or in pairs.

ICT was an essential part of Challenge 2000 – it was not only the medium through which the challenge was presented to pupils, but it also offered ways of finding out information and presenting data collected from various sources.

In addition to *Help* buttons on the Web pages for additional information relating to the challenge questions, pupils within the same LEA could send an email for help to the 'mission controller' of the balloon flight (Mr Jones) if they were stuck. They received a reply giving additional clues or suggestions, but no answers!

The two originators of Challenge 2000 (Mr Jones and Mr Rogers) prepared the content for the challenges; this content had had to be transferred into Web page format (html) to go on the LEA Grid for Learning, so Mr Jones and Mr Rogers had had to learn how to do this in the early stages of the project. Because the LEA Web site was managed by Research Machines (RM) under the Public Private Partnership (PPP) contract, the initial Challenge 2000 materials had had to be checked and tested by RM to ensure they would run effectively. Once the LEA had adopted the material, and realised that it could be shared more widely via an 'outward facing' Web site as well as the 'inward facing' intranet, a webmaster was nominated to manage the transfer of the content onto the Internet. The webmaster was a member of the Research Machines team already working with the LEA as part of its PPP project to install and maintain ICT services within schools in the authority.

4.3.3 Teacher practices and outcomes

The innovation teacher supervised pupils working on the innovation for two sessions during the school week, as well as during four sessions held after school. She commented on how Challenge 2000 had provided the children with more breadth and depth than the National Curriculum alone could provide: *'It covers so much of the curriculum and the idea is a world wide vision. Children couldn't have got that from any other resources.'*

She went on to say,

> *The biggest change has been flexibility. We feel that we don't have to justify Challenge 2000 because it fulfils the National Curriculum...the children teach me things which gives me a better relationship with them.*

The studio environment allowed the teacher to observe the dynamics of each group without detracting from their independent learning. We observed the teacher moving around the room, checking on each group's progress and offering advice and support where necessary. She did not think that her approach to classroom management and instruction had changed, although she felt that the innovation had shifted the responsibility for managing pupils' activities away from her to the pupils themselves.

The teacher said that her role had changed from instructor to facilitator and that this had given her the opportunity to assess the pupils' progress and group interactions informally, without having '*to hover over them at all times*'. Other teachers and the LEA adviser commented that the role of the teacher had changed and had become '*largely advisory*'. The LEA adviser stated:

> *When they're working with Challenge 2000 their role has changed. They're not taking the lead, the children are, and the teacher is the facilitator, which can be strange because they're no longer the expert.*

A parent had noticed that there was '*more independent study rather than teacher-based*'. She went on to say:

> *The resources are all they need to answer the questions. The teacher is there to help and give hints, but they don't give them the answers. They want them to find as many ways as they can to find the answer.*

The innovation teacher explained that she had not needed any extra training to fulfil her role in the innovation effectively. The headteacher agreed, saying that all teachers needed was '*to be able to use a PC and a search engine*'. The innovation did, however, require collaboration between staff and adults outside of the school: the originators collaborated with others who suggested and drafted material to include within different stages of the challenge. The innovation teacher herself had collaborated with one of the originators of Challenge 2000 to write the second challenge, which took the balloon to France.

4.3.4 Student practices and outcomes

The Challenge 2000 material brought together aspects of different curricula areas together with wider aspects of general knowledge, cultural awareness and problem-solving. Pupils were encouraged to draw on a variety of resources when attempting to solve the problems: during the sessions we observed encyclopaedias, atlases (see photo 10) and dictionaries being used frequently, in addition to pupils searching for information on the Internet.

The number of questions posed in each month's challenge forced pupils to sub-divide their groups in order to work effectively. The guidelines for pupils stated:

Don't try and solve all problems with your group – it's not possible – unless you've got an extra twelve months! You need to share out the tasks – know the 'pages' you are responsible for and get on with it.

Teachers, pupils and parents acknowledged that this 'teamwork' approach of allocating specific tasks to different members of the group was different from the usual approach to group work in the classroom, where pupils could be ostensibly working in a group, but actually engaged in the same tasks when sitting together. One pupil commented:

We normally work in pairs on a computer, so Challenge 2000 taught us to work as a team, which is better because we have more people's ideas. Different people have different strengths, such as practical strengths as well as computer strengths.

Teachers, pupils and parents identified numerous positive impacts of Challenge 2000:

Positive impacts

♦ **motivation**: pupils were keen to work on Challenge 2000 in their own time (before and after school) as well as during the timetabled sessions; pupils commented that they liked '*solving questions*'; '*learning more about other countries*'; and '*learning something new each day*'; the headteacher noted, '*The children are excited about this project and that has an effect on the rest of their work, which will affect their achievement*' and the innovation teacher stated '*They don't have a problem maintaining motivation and excitement*';

♦ **discipline**: the teamwork approach had helped to improve pupils' self-discipline;

♦ **attendance**: attendance for Year 6 had gone up and had remained higher than before Challenge 2000;

♦ **improved ICT skills**: pupils were more confident and more skilled in using PCs, to the extent that the school was considering seeking formal accreditation of their skills;

♦ **better general knowledge**: parents noted their children had improved their general knowledge; one commented '*I'm convinced that there are things he could only have learnt through Challenge 2000*';

♦ **independent learning**: the teacher acted as a facilitator; the pupils had to organise the efforts of their group effectively and decide on the strategies they would use to find out information;

♦ **personal and social benefits**: personal confidence and effective 'teamworking' skills were mentioned; one boy admitted, '*I found it hard to work in groups before Year 6, but now I'm good at it*' – another pupil agreed with this view. One of the originators stated, '*It's interesting to see groups gelling and the different talents emerging. Those who may be seen as less able have made great contributions which have stunned the rest of the group, and they are now seen as valued contributors.*'

Pupils were involved in two new activities arising from their work on Challenge 2000:

New activities

1. **using a shared area of the network**: the innovation teacher explained, '*They work in groups, but simultaneously on PCs, using shared areas – this is the only occasion that they use shared areas*';

2. **they contact external 'experts' for specialist information**: we observed an example of this when two boys left the studio to telephone the local branch of the territorial army to ask about how to survive in the desert (the context was that their balloon had crash-landed in the Sahara Desert). Some minutes later they returned and reported that they had to fax an enquiry. The teacher told the boys to draft one; they automatically started using Word to do this.

4.4   Case Study – Secondary 1

Highgrove High School – *'Turning potential into performance'*: using a database to record, monitor and set targets for student performance throughout a secondary school

4.4.1   Curriculum content, goals and assessment

Highgrove High School had designed the structure of its own computer database to record performance data and targets for all its students (approximately 1900 aged 11–18 years) in all subjects. The data collected formed a basis for detailed analyses by subject/year/teaching group. Thus the innovation was directly related to assessment, but the information in the database was used formatively, as well as summatively, to improve teaching and learning, as it provided information which could be used to determine the different ability teaching groups (sets) and could influence how teachers delivered lesson content.

Within each department, a curriculum coordinator was responsible for ensuring that teachers entered the grades for student achievement and effort for the classes they taught: *'There are machines for staff to use and for them to enter the assessment grades'*, *'Staff put the achievement and effort grade in the boxes'*. This information could be analysed by Heads of Department to monitor student attainment and also by Heads of Year who maintained an overview of students' performance across subjects. Details of achievement in all subjects were supplemented by test scores in national tests as well as tests designed to indicate students' future performance potential.

The school used tests designed to measure students' ability (rather than achievement) to predict their academic achievements in subsequent examinations. Students sat the NFER-Nelson Cognitive Abilities Tests (CAT) tests in Years 7 and 9: these measured ability in verbal reasoning, quantitative reasoning and non-verbal reasoning and gave an indication of their potential performance in the mandatory tests in English, mathematics and science at the end of Year 9. In addition, students sat the YELLIS[13] tests in Year 10, which were designed to give an indication of student performance in their 16+ examinations in Year 11 (GSCE). They also sat ALIS tests in Year 12 to give an indication of performance in examinations at 18+ (A-level academic courses and GNVQ vocational courses). One teacher commented, *'We get NFER, YELLIS, estimated and predicted grades, all the data is there in the machines…'*

Although many secondary schools use a database for recording assessment data of this type, this particular example was innovatory because of the detail of the information involved, the degree of accessibility of the data to staff,

---

[13] The YELLIS and ALIS tests are offered by the University of Durham: schools that subscribe to the service are provided with tests to administer to students. The completed tests are analysed at Durham, and information showing the predicted grades for each student is returned to the school. More information can be found at http://cem.dur.ac.uk/yellis and http://cem.dur.ac.uk/alis.

and the fact that much activity, including various forms of target setting, took place upon the basis of these data. Highgrove High School had progressed beyond the mere collection of data (which is in itself not particularly useful or innovatory) to a stage of actively utilising the information. Underlying the use of the student-tracking database was the school's desire to enable all students to achieve their potential: the headteacher stated the aim of the database was to '*improve pupil performance*' and another teacher said, '*We know which students we can make a difference with – turning potential into performance. We can use the data to set realistic targets and keep parents informed and involved*'.

Within the school, the database had resulted in a change from summative assessment, with reports going to parents twice per year, to ongoing assessment which was formative because the detailed information about the students in their teaching groups allowed teachers to structure courses and prepare lessons more effectively. One teacher stated '*We're all aware of a major reorientation – ongoing reflection about performance rather than just checking what students have achieved at the end of the year. Monitoring and evaluation are more real*'; another commented on the ability '*...to create different pathways through a project for particular students*'.

4.4.2 Kinds of technology and ways they are used

The student-tracking database was operated using a Claris Filemaker Pro v3 database which had been structured to allow easy entry and retrieval of relevant data. This was run on the school's local area network. Senior managers (the headteacher, three Deputy Heads, most Heads of Year and some Heads of Department) had their own desktop computer (either Mac or PC) linked to the network, four computers were available to all staff within the lower school staffroom and four more were available on the upper school site. The school had a licence for a maximum of 15 users accessing Filemaker at any one time. A fibre-optic cable provided a network link between the two geographically separate sites (the lower school and the upper school).

Whilst Heads of Year all had access to their own desktop computer (either Mac or PC) which enabled them to access the student-tracking database, some of the teachers who were expected to enter data did not have access to their own machine. These teachers either had to use computers in communal areas to enter data, or had to borrow a colleague's machine to do this. As a result, some of these teachers did not enter data promptly and subject coordinators and/or Heads of Year had to remind them to do so; one subject coordinator commented '*It's hard work to go round and get other people to enter data, it's quicker to enter the data myself.*'

Teachers commented that it would not be possible to keep so much information about individual students without using the database:

> *We still need to keep a paper-based record system, but we wouldn't have the range of information without IT. There is no way I could keep records on 330 students across six tests per year, plus an end-of-year exam, plus two reports with effort and attainment grades (the grades are moderated within the department).*

It's good to scan overall performance [on one screen display] *rather than 12 sheets of paper* [one record sheet for each of twelve subjects for each of approximately 20 students].

4.4.3   Teacher practices and outcomes

Teachers had different levels of involvement with the student-tracking database, according to their responsibilities: subject teachers were expected to enter the grades for all students in the classes they taught; Heads of Year, Heads of Department and other senior managers could access the database to monitor students' performance. One Head of Year stated '*Staff put the achievement grade and effort grade in the boxes...It's the responsibility of subject teachers to put in marks, to put grades on the computer.*'

Teachers had to be able to input data and those with managerial roles needed to know how to analyse the data. Training was therefore given at different levels: '*I was shown in ten minutes how to input the data; since then I've been able to input the data, I think it's quite straightforward*'; '*There are things you can do but I didn't realise, so I asked* [a deputy head]'; teachers also mentioned key stage staff meetings focusing on the student-tracking database.

Numerous comments were made about the information stored in the student-tracking database giving teachers a better insight into individual students' capabilities and enabling them to identify strengths and weaknesses: '*If a child has 8 A's and a D in something I could call a child in and talk about the problem. I can spot anomalies/problems very quickly*'; '*Having more information available is very useful – it saves time; it has enabled a clearer focus on individuals*'.

Heads of Year felt that this increased knowledge extended their role from being predominantly pastoral to monitoring students' achievement across subjects. One stated '*The system brings together the academic and pastoral roles. The role of Head of Year becomes mentor rather than policeman.*' Another commented:

I know more about them, there's now more linking with the curriculum side rather than just telling them off for being naughty. Now I know whether they are good in English/mathematics/across subjects.

The student-tracking database information was also utilised during consultations with parents and/or students as it provided evidence relating to student performance.

Teachers reported using the data to guide their teaching practices (e.g. using verbal reasoning scores to identify students whose literacy skills needed developing) and to prepare their lessons more effectively. Some teachers mentioned creating different routes through a project for students with different capabilities and using the data to decide on the approach used and the pace of the lesson. Others cited using the data for determining different teaching sets based on student ability.

It gives a profile of the group – this helps you decide how to pitch the delivery of a lesson, how to pace it. For example, I would use a different approach if all students are level 6 and above in the KS3 national tests[14].

Several teachers stated that their involvement with the student-tracking database had improved their personal understanding of and competence in ICT.

Although the student-tracking database had been developed within the school, a software development consultant had played an important role by providing training in the Claris Filemaker program for the Head of ICT and the Head of Key Stage 3. The consultant had worked closely with the Head of ICT to develop a structure for the database that reflected the school organisation and to help set up the various fields within it.

4.4.4   Student practices and outcomes

The student-tracking database was used throughout the school to record achievement and effort grades in all subjects for all students. It was also used with older students to record the minimum grades in subject examinations that students should aim for: target minimum grades (TMGs). In Year 11 students sat the GCSE and in Year 13 students could enter for a range of different qualifications: AS and A2 (academic) and VCE (vocational). At key points within students' secondary education, data from mandatory and other tests were added to the database. Students were involved in the tracking database when their performance was reviewed by a teacher – either a subject teacher, or their Head of Year who monitored students' performance across subjects. Appendix V shows the use of the student-tracking database throughout the school.

Students were involved in the use of the tracking database in the following ways:

Tracking database

♦ Generally, in Years 7, 8 and 9 (KS3) students' performance was monitored and teachers discussed any problems (such as unusually poor results) with individual students.

♦ Teachers set TMGs for students' GCSEs in Year 11 (KS4), using YELLIS predictions; they may/may not have discussed these TMGs with the students.

♦ In Year 12 (KS5), students had an interview with each subject teacher to discuss their TMG for the courses they would complete in Year 13; the TMGs were initially based on ALIS predictions, but were subsequently modified later in Year 12 and in Year 13 on the basis of (a) students' ongoing performance, and (b) the grades required by higher education institutions.

Because teachers discussed individual students' performance and (where appropriate) TMGs with them, students had more information about their potential and could work to improve areas of weakness and achieve higher grades. One teacher commented '[at A-level] *they think about what they can*

---

[14] The national tests are mandatory in maintained schools, and are attempted by students at the end of key stages. Pupils sit the tests at the end of Key Stage 1 (primary, age seven years), Key Stage 2 (primary, age 11 years) and Key Stage 3 (secondary, age 14 years). According to their performance in these tests, students are deemed to have reached different levels of attainment (from level 1 to level 8, followed by 'exceptional').

do to improve themselves'. Another remarked:

> *It develops the positive attitude and makes students aim for a higher future career. If I asked pupils to go to the library to pull up their grades, they won't do that, but if I show them this data then it gives them a boost and makes them want to improve their grades. I've certainly found this at KS5.*

The tracking database was also seen as a contributory factor in raising standards and increasing enrolment in the sixth form (KS5):

> *The structure* [of the student-tracking database] *proved effective in improving results. An advantage was self-evident to teachers, students and the parents ... It's not totally responsible for the improvement in achievement, but it is a large part of it.*

> *Students who benefit most are probably those who are underachieving, because their performance is being monitored – it's making sense of assessment: students have to confront the data regarding their underachievement. Partly because of our system, our results have improved dramatically* [leading to] *approx 400 in the sixth form* [i.e. students were more likely to continue their studies beyond age 16].

Evidence of the improvement in students' performance can be seen in the school's published results for students in examinations at 16+, shown in Table 2 below. Of course, the enhanced student achievement is most likely to be a result of a combination of factors, rather than any one factor, although, as stated above, teachers felt that the student-tracking database had contributed to this overall improvement.

Table 4.4.4.1: Percentage of students achieving national target of at least five passes at GCSE at grades A*–C (or GNVQ equivalent)

	Highgrove High School		LEA average	National average
	5 or more passes	No passes	(5 or more passes)	(5 or more passes)
Year	%	%	%	%
1996	39	3	35	44
1997	47	2	38	45
1998	57	3	45	46
1999	54	1	43	48
2000	60	0	47	49
2001	55	0	46	50

Students were aware that their teachers monitored their performance by accessing the data in the student-tracking database; some felt that they should have been allowed to access the data relating to their own achievement themselves. Finally, some parents also supported student and/or parental access to their own children's details, but a number of teachers expressed concerns that students with low TMGs would be de-motivated.

Photo 1 – Windmill Primary School

The main Year 6 classroom; additional workstations were located in an annexe to the main classroom.

Photo 2 – Windmill Primary School

Every workstation has headphones and speakers: pupils use them if appropriate for the work they are doing.

Photo 3 – Windmill Primary School

A typical piece of pupils' work on display: a word processed report of a science investigation, including digital photographs, diagrams of equipment prepared using a drawing package, and results presented using a spreadsheet.

Photo 4 – Windmill Primary School

The innovation teacher using the data projector to illustrate how pupils will receive automated feedback from their daily mental arithmetic tests.

Photo 5 – Woodford Junior School

One of the Year 6 girls drafting her email to her E-pal using Word.

Photo 6 – Woodford Junior School

One of the Year 6 boys drafting a message to his E-pal using Word.

Photo 7 – Moorcroft Primary School

The display board for recording the progress of the balloons.

Photo 8 – Moorcroft Primary School

The innovation teacher with some of the Year 6 pupils in the multi-purpose studio.

Photo 9 – Moorcroft Primary School

Pupils used on-line atlases as well as conventional printed atlases.

Photo 10 – Moorcroft Primary School

The innovation teacher helping a boy with a geographical question.

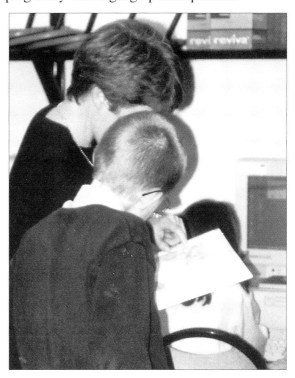

Photo 11 – Coleridge College

Year 10 students working on the on-line GNVQ at a Tuesday 15:00-17:00hrs session in one of the three adjacent ICT suites.

Photo 12 – Coleridge College

Year 10 students working on the on-line GNVQ at a Tuesday 15:00-17:00hrs session. Glazed partitions divide the three adjacent ICT suites; the two outer suites are allocated to the on-line course and the middle suite is usually allocated to students attending the school's 'homework club' – an opportunity to use the computers to assist them with their work. There is one laser printer in each suite.

Photo 13 – Coleridge College

Year 10 students working on the on-line GNVQ at a Wednesday 15:00-16:00hrs session in the English hub. There is one laser printer for the 15 machines in the hub.

Photo 14 – Coleridge College

Year 10 students working on the on-line GNVQ at a Wednesday 15:00-16:00hrs session in the English hub. The teacher moves around the class assisting individual students as necessary.

Photo 15 – Belgrove High School

Two students using the Picture Tel video-conferencing equipment in an office at the rear of one of the MFL classrooms.

Photo 16 – Belgrove High School

Two Year 11 students using the Swift Site video-conferencing equipment, which was also connected to a video-recorder, allowing the innovation teacher to record the sessions. This was set up in the innovation teacher's office.

4.5   Case Study – Secondary 2

Coleridge College – A two-year on-line course leading to accreditation in ICT at 16+

4.5.1   Curriculum content, goals and assessment

The innovation was a two-year on-line course run as an after-school option, leading to formal accreditation in ICT at age 16 (a General National Vocational Qualification (GNVQ) intermediate award). The on-line GNVQ course covered the same content as the time-tabled GNVQ course offered to Year 12 students. However, it differed in that it was offered to Year 10 students outside school hours, used the materials devised by Walton High School and had far less teacher input than the traditional course. The content of the on-line course, such as multimedia resources and the various course assignments, had been prepared by Walton High School; the course was presented as six units, one per term for the full two-year course. Walton High School posted the course materials on their own Web site, which students could access by using a password, and onto CD-ROMs at a rate of one unit per term, and Coleridge College installed the units from the CD-ROM onto its intranet as they were released. Teachers at Coleridge were responsible for supporting students experiencing difficulty, supervising sessions and marking coursework according to the guidelines for assessing students' work provided by the examination board; the guidelines were supplemented by examples of students' work supplied by Walton High. The assessment criteria for the on-line GNVQ course were the same as for the standard course, because both were determined by the examination board. One teacher described the course as follows:

> *The key difference is the level of motivation of students in an after-school session – there is higher personal motivation. They are left to their own devices to a much greater degree. Clearly you want to let them be independent... The teaching time is less.*

Sessions took place in the ICT computer rooms (see photos 11 and 12) and in the English hub (see photos 13 and 14), where students could work individually with access to the resources they needed (e.g. headphones, Walton High materials, printers).

The objective of the course was to enable students to leave school with an extra qualification – a GNVQ in IT that would be regarded as equivalent to four GCSE passes. The principal explained that the aim of providing this course was to encourage students to think about their future careers and offer 'borderline' students (those who were likely to achieve fewer than five GCSE passes at grades A*–C) a chance to gain extra qualifications. The course was seen as beneficial because it meant students were responsible for their own learning and they could work at their own pace.

4.5.2   Kinds of technology and ways they are used

The on-line course required one PC workstation per student: this meant that groups of students had to be allocated to specific computer rooms where there were at least as many PCs as students. The computers needed as a minimum a Pentium 166 MHz processor, 64 MB RAM and a sound card. The following were also essential: Microsoft Windows 95 (or later) and Microsoft Office 97 (or later), and Real Player (for the video sequences). The course materials were loaded onto the school's intranet, but hyperlinks within the materials meant that Internet access was also required.

The school workstations needed headphones for each student (teachers took these to the sessions and students plugged them in); a printer was essential for providing hard copies of the students' work. The school computer rooms had one fast laser printer per suite of approximately 16 machines.

Students were expected to do one hour of study for the course in addition to the school-based session(s) each week: this could be done either at home, or at the school when computers were available for private study (e.g. the school ran a homework club Tuesday–Thursday 3–4pm). Students could access the course materials in the following ways:

Access to
course materials

♦   via the school intranet

♦   at home, via the Internet: students were provided with a user name and password to access the Walton High School course via their Web site

♦   at home, using a CD-ROM which had all the materials for one unit.

One teacher also explained how students stored their work electronically:

> *To my knowledge* [all] *students have 50MB of space on the network ... Some are doing GCSE IT as well, so some can organise their own folders. Some hadn't used computers before they came to Coleridge College so I gave them support and showed them how to create sub-folders.*

4.5.3   Teacher practices and outcomes

The on-line GNVQ ICT course had been provided by another secondary school (Walton High), where staff had developed the materials in accordance with the examination board syllabus, used them with its own students and subsequently offered them to selected other schools, including Coleridge College. The course coordinator at Coleridge had had to attend a compulsory training day each term at Walton High School: this introduced the content for the next unit of the course. The teachers at Coleridge did not prepare any of the course content, although several remarked that they would like to collate a bank of real examples of documents such as faxes and invoices, rather than relying on students using the examples provided in the on-line materials, or trying to obtain examples from other sources.

Teachers involved in the on-line GNVQ supervised the students, who worked at their own pace using the computers. All five teachers running the course taught ICT courses within the college, four as their main subject and one in addition to mathematics. However, because the on-line course provided all the teaching and learning materials, there was general agreement that specialist ICT skills were not necessary to teach the course. As all teachers running the course taught ICT, this made it easy for them to liaise informally about the course, monitoring progress and identifying issues for discussion.

The teacher's role was very different from the usual; those running the course stated their role was that of a facilitator: '*My role is more of facilitator than teacher – helping them when they get stuck*'; '*It's more of a facilitator role*'. There was much less teacher–student interaction because the focus of learning had moved from the teacher to the computers – teachers did not deliver the lesson, instead they assisted individual students with any problems that arose as they were using the on-line course materials. Students also noted the different approach: '*The course is different because it is not taught by a teacher.*'

Because the entire session involved students working independently, most teacher–student interactions were on a one-to-one basis, although teachers commented that they would normally do this during traditional lessons: '*I aim to talk to every student during the lesson and would do that regardless of the type of lesson*'; '*It's normal practice to support on a one-to-one basis as they are working.*'

The college had been running the GNVQ ICT course using traditional teaching methods before the on-line course was introduced, so some of those teaching the course had previous experience of the course content to draw upon, although they had had to become familiar with the on-line course materials. Teachers contrasted the instructional approach used in the on-line GNVQ ICT course with the traditional GNVQ ICT course that the college had run in previous years, and was still running for students in Year 12: '*It's the same syllabus as before, but with integrated resources use. It's more appealing because of the multimedia approach.*' The teachers also commented that the course requirement of one computer for every student was different from the approach they adopted during GCSE IT courses, where the greater number of students meant that lessons had to have two main activities:

> *In the IT suites, we tend to have 18 PCs in each room (rooms C1–C5) which means that GCSE classes have to share or split the class in half, so that half are using PCs and the others are writing. This caused problems for the after-school course because we can't get all students in the room with a machine each. GSCE courses* [25–30 students per class] *spend half their time doing written work. That's one of the reasons for having the on-line GNVQ after school. GNVQ requires a 1-1 student:machine ratio* [which has been achieved].

The teachers commented positively about being involved in the on-line course: '*…it is genuinely an innovation. I wanted to do it because it's a new thing of the future*'; '*…seeing a new method of teaching*'; '*It's new to us as teachers, so it's also exciting to us*'.

4.5.4 Student practices and outcomes

Students who volunteered for the course attended sessions after school (either one two-hour session or two one-hour sessions per week). The course was offered to all Year 10 students (i.e. those entering the school), and about 20 per cent (105 students) had registered for the course. Students accessed the multimedia on-line course materials and carried out tasks for the assignments for each unit of the course (two assignments per unit). All students had one-to-one access to a PC, and worked independently at their own pace, although they had to submit the assignments for each unit by the specified deadline.

Both teachers and parents commented that students were motivated and enjoying the course. Students noted that they had more independence as compared with traditional lessons: '*I like the independence, the sense of responsibility for my own education.*'

One teacher commented that students '...*have to adapt to the way the content is delivered, e.g. wearing headphones, looking at what to do and writing down tasks.*' Another summarised the course structure as follows:

Course structure

The key pattern is that [for each unit] *they:*

1. read/watch on screen

2. compose (typing or researching)

3. prepare evidence

4. submit the assignment for assessment.

Another teacher described the types of student activities using the on-line course:

At the moment we have worked on the first couple of assignments. The first one was to do with types of documents, e.g. what is an invoice, agenda, newspaper or flyer. They have to find other examples of these documents and evaluate them. Lots of them knew what a newspaper was, but not an agenda so they followed hyperlinks or searched [using search engines] *for what it was and found it. Students helped each other out and talked to each other a lot.*

The second one is to watch a real video and make minutes of it and then they are given tasks to do for the school's 'Fame' production. They use whatever software they want to produce these things.

There was widespread agreement that students on the course were benefiting in a number of ways, including:

Benefits to students

♦ **greater access to ICT**: this was mentioned as a particular benefit to those students who had not opted to study GCSE ICT;

♦ **opportunities to develop the ICT skills** that they would need in the future, both in an educational context and when seeking employment;

- **the opportunity to repeat sections** of the content if they did not understand it first time;

- **experience of an approach which required self-motivation** and an ability to pace their own work: the autonomous style of learning was seen as useful preparation for students who went on to study courses at A-level and at university;

- **the course led to a formal qualification in ICT**: a GNVQ intermediate level award, which is equivalent to four GCSE passes at grades A*–C.

Although students worked at the tasks at their own pace, they could compare their ideas and approaches with other students. One commented: '*We work more closely with other students and have more help from them than in other lessons*'; another stated '*We help each other more, get information from someone else. If I'm stuck I would first ask the person next to me and then Mr X* [the teacher]'.

4.6 Case Study – Secondary 3

Belgrove High School – Using video-conferencing to improve English students' conversational skills in French in Year 11

4.6.1 Curriculum content, goals and assessment

Belgrove High School was a language college and all students studied two modern foreign languages to the end of Year 11. The school was well-equipped with ICT resources and the policy throughout the modern foreign languages (MFL) department was that one in every five lessons must be ICT-based. One way in which ICT enhanced MFL work was through video-conferencing sessions, which provided students with opportunities to practise their conversational skills in a modern foreign language. The focus of the research was the video-conferencing work organised for some Year 11 students (aged 15–16 years) over a ten-week period from January to April, leading up to the oral examinations for GCSE during May. Forty-minute sessions took place on four days per week (Monday, Tuesday, Thursday and Friday) during lunch times: 12.20pm – 1.00pm. During this time, two groups of two or three students took part in a video-conferencing session with two or three students in France, each group having a session of approximately 20 minutes. Within each session students spent about half of the time talking in French, and about half of the time in English: this allowed students in both countries to take part in a conversation with a native speaker of another language.

The innovation teacher and the teacher in France liaised to produce the following programme of ten topics, a different one for each week:

Topics

1. **On se présente** – introducing yourself (personal information)

2. **Les passetemps** – free time and entertainment

3. **A la maison** – house and home

4. **A l'école** – school (differences between French and English schools)

5. **La ville et la région** – town and region

6. **L'argent** – money

7. **Manger et boire** – food and drink

8. **Les vacances** – holidays

9. **Projets d'avenir** – future plans

10. **La santé** – healthy diet, smoking, drinking, etc.

The ten topics reflected the content of the syllabus that students followed during their normal class lessons. During the 2000–01 school year, for the first time, the innovation teacher had prepared more detailed worksheets for each session, giving a list of ten sample questions that students might use during the video-conferencing session. These worksheets were intended to guide the conversation and ensure that the students did not remain silent because they could not think of anything to ask.

The innovation teacher reported:

> *The aims are to develop oral skills, fluency, listening skills, also accent and intonation, and cultural insight and* [to] *extend the best students. It fits in with the gifted and talented initiative. The current syllabus is very vocabulary heavy, so it's difficult to stretch talented pupils.*

By improving students' conversational skills, video-conferencing sessions were intended to assist students' preparation for their oral examination.

Teachers and students reported that the lunchtime video-conferencing sessions were quite relaxed, partly because the students had volunteered for them and because there was no teacher present; however, this also posed problems relating to assessment. Our observations found that some students chose to record the French students' responses to their questions on the worksheet, but others did not. The innovation teacher described the ways that he collected information about what had taken place during the sessions:

> *We're now videoing what we do. I'm setting up the technology to know what they're doing during the video-conferencing. I can make use of this with classes, parents, etc. The answers on the sheets give me some assessment of how they've got on, but they might not have done that. I have stood outside the door and listened. Some of my best moments in teaching have been through listening to some of my students during the video-conferencing – having a conversation, laughing, or having a serious debate.*

He went on to explain how he wanted the video-conferencing sessions to contribute to other lessons:

> *What I'm moving towards is having closer links between what happens in the video-conferencing sessions and the classroom – prepared in advance, and followed up. The rest of the class could ask questions of those involved in video-conferencing, so the rest of the class gets the experience as well .... I'd like a freer hand in Year 11, and base the entire programme around the video-conferencing. The exam syllabus is a constraint.*

4.6.2 Kinds of technology and ways they are used

There were four sets of equipment for video-conferencing: three of these were PC based, using Picture Tel Link 2000 software together with a remote control camera, microphone and speakers. Two of these systems were located in small offices at the back of two language classrooms (see photo 15), and a third was in the annexe used for ICT-based language lessons. Having the equipment located in separate rooms meant that the students were away from the rest of the class, so they were less self-conscious; the headteacher also noted, *'Acoustically it's better ...with a small space than a larger one.'* The fourth system used Swift Site connected to a TV, again with camera, microphone and speakers. A video recorder was connected to the Swift Site system so that the teacher could make recordings of the video-conferencing sessions (see photo 16). All four systems used ISDN2 lines.

Teachers were aware that video-conferencing could be arranged via the Internet, but commented that the sound quality was less good and there were greater time delays in the visual images. Although the focus was on speaking and listening skills, teachers and students reported that the visual link between the students was also important, as non-verbal communication contributed to understanding on both sides. One of the Year 11 students remarked, *'If we get things wrong we can see them laughing, but if you can't see them you don't know if you've got it wrong.'* It was perhaps because of the value of non-verbal cues that earlier attempts to encourage conversational skills by using phones had been less successful and had stopped.

The video-conferencing equipment available in the school was sufficient for the sessions the school was involved in, although some teachers indicated that if more equipment were available, it would allow students to participate more frequently in video-conferencing sessions during lesson time.

Both the headteacher and the innovation teacher stressed the role of technology in allowing students to communicate with native French speakers, with the former commenting, *'You do it in a technological way or don't do it. There isn't a non-technological alternative.'*

4.6.3   Teacher practices and outcomes

The MFL teachers were involved in setting up each of the video-conferencing sessions, either during lessons or in lunchtime. This involved establishing the computer link via the ISDN2 line, positioning the camera effectively for the visual link using the remote control, and putting the microphone in place; one system (Swift Site) involved connections via a television rather than a PC. Teachers had had to use a range of organisational skills to set up and run the sessions. For regular lessons, teachers had to manage their class whilst allowing for students to leave the room to participate in the video-conferencing sessions. For the voluntary lunchtime sessions, the innovation teacher had to plan and organise an effective programme for the ten-week course, independent of the main curriculum lessons for all students.

Teachers from both countries collaborated on the topics to be addressed during each session, and prepared worksheets covering a number of questions on each topic. Students then prepared sample responses to these questions before the video-conferencing session. As one MFL teacher said:

> *Staff are on hand if they need them, but they can get on with it* [video-conferencing] *without a teacher looking over their shoulder –* [it] *shows trust on the part of the teacher.*

The teacher's role had changed in that the students were learning with other students. The innovation teacher also found that his role now involved forging and maintaining links with other schools and teachers, as well as higher education institutions, with the aim of setting up further video-conferencing opportunities. The LEA adviser for ICT commented on the teacher's role, saying:

> *What they're aiming to do is develop student skills as well as other things. To develop their* [students'] *horizons, so that they know there are different students out there.*

The video-conferencing had forced the innovation teacher to alter his classroom management strategies. He commented that his 'approach has to have changed to accommodate these activities and I do encourage independent learning more'. The vision of teaching and learning, both of the school and the MFL teachers, was to promote and encourage independent learning. He went on to say:

> I'm not making sure they do certain things, which is different to having your own agenda in the classroom. As far as the pupils in my class are concerned, I have seen another side to them, which is very positive, using [their] initiative.

All the MFL teachers said that the video-conferencing had made an impact on their teaching practice. The innovation teacher said:

> I've gained technical expertise and confidence to explore other developments. It's widened my horizons...given me access and insight into other ways of doing things. I've written a chapter for a book with the headteacher, which has been in several journals, and I have been asked to speak at various places.

Despite these positive impacts on teachers, there were some barriers that had to be overcome, such as timetabling issues with partner schools that affected the scheduling of the sessions.

4.6.4   Student practices and outcomes

Students participated in weekly video-conferencing sessions with students in France; each session lasted about 20 minutes (ten minutes in French, with the French students asking the questions and the English students responding in French, and ten minutes in English, with the English students asking the questions and the French students responding in English). The sessions were organised so that students video-conferenced with the same partners each week: this was intended to help students get to know each other and feel more at ease. The conversations between the students were guided by a different topic for each week's session, with a worksheet listing ten typical questions for each topic (see section 4.6.1; we saw students using questions on *La santé* – see Appendix VI). The innovation teacher viewed the worksheets as an aid to preparation for each session. Students received the worksheets in the lesson before the session so that they could think about their own answers to these questions, and other related questions to ask the French students. The worksheets could also be used as a means for students to record the French students' responses to the questions.

Students in the two classes representing the top set (of three ability sets) were invited to volunteer for the lunchtime video-conferencing sessions. The innovation teacher explained:

> I'd like to be able to offer it to everyone but they have to have a certain level of language skills to be able to carry it out... For the less able it would have to be a one-off, whereas for this level you have to be able to maintain the conversation from week to week.

Modern foreign language teachers reported using a variety of strategies to develop students' speaking and listening skills during their lessons, such as role-playing in small groups, and conversations with the teacher and the French *assistante*. Teachers and students commented on the differences between these activities and the video-conferencing sessions: *'In the class they're playing a role in the dialogue, but in the video-conferencing they're themselves...It's more natural ...It's more relaxed because there is no teacher ...'*; *'...in a classroom, it's artificial and with video-conferencing you're talking to them in their own language – authenticity'*; and *'because we don't know them, there's more to ask them.'*

Teachers, parents and students reported that students had benefited from improvements in their listening and speaking skills, their French accent and confidence as well as gaining cultural insights. The headteacher explained that video-conferencing gave the students *'... access to formal and slightly less formal French – different types of discourse which are not immediately available with traditional learning.'*

The school had also collaborated with two separate research institutions in studies to collect and analyse data relating to students who had participated in the video-conferencing. The results of both studies suggested that the video-conferencing had a positive impact on student achievement in the formal GCSE examination (see Appendix VII).

Concluding remarks

This chapter has presented the main findings from the six case studies carried out in England. The clear message emerging from this research concerns not the importance of ICTs in their own right, but the benefits to be gained when confident teachers are willing to explore new opportunities for changing their classroom practices by utilising ICT.

The full case reports on the six schools studied in England can be viewed and downloaded from the NFER website: www.nfer.ac.uk.

GLOSSARY

A and AS-levels	Advanced level and Advanced Subsidiary courses: 17/18+ courses.
AAL	Anytime Anywhere Learning, a scheme introduced by Microsoft to promote student access to laptop computers so that students can use them at school and at home to support their learning.
Advanced Skills Teacher	Teachers with specialist skills in teaching a particular subject. These teachers receive extra remuneration and have to spend part of their time sharing their expertise with colleagues. See also www.dfee.gov.uk/ast/
ALIS	A-level indicator system. See also www.cem.dur.ac.uk/alis
BITC	Business in the Community: a national organisation with regional officers that encourages businesses to become involved in the activities of the local community, including local schools. See www.bitc.org.uk
CAT	Cognitive Abilities Tests – these measure ability in verbal reasoning, quantitative reasoning and non-verbal reasoning. See also www.nfer-nelson.co.uk/cat/index.htm
Community College	Some schools are designated 'community' schools/colleges. These provide access to the facilities at the school for use by the local community, sometimes during but more usually outside school hours (e.g. badminton courts; hall). Additional staff usually organise/run the community activities within the school. At Belgrove, two teachers within the MFL department each had a 0.5 teaching commitment and a 0.5 commitment to promoting effective community links.
Cross-curricular	An approach intended to support and/or draw in different areas of the curriculum, including English, mathematics, history, geography and religious education. The term may be applied to resources that pupils use and/or work that pupils engage in. This approach to teaching and learning is also sometimes called a 'thematic' or 'topic' approach.

Director of Sixth Form Studies	A teacher with responsibility for managing the teaching programme within Years 12 and 13.
Epal	The name given to either partner in a two-way link between pupils at Woodford Junior School and employees at the Ericsson factory nearby. Each pupil in the project was linked with one employee at Ericsson. The partners communicated with each other by email.
GCSE	General Certificate of Secondary Education: an assessment at age 16+ consisting of both examination and assessed coursework.
GNVQ	General National Vocational Qualification: a 16+ qualification that has a more vocational emphasis than the GSCE.
Head of Department	The most senior teacher within a department; s/he has managerial responsibilities for that curriculum area (e.g. Head of English).
Head of Year	A teacher who is responsible for overseeing the work and progress of all classes or students in one year (e.g. Head of Year 7; Head of Year 8).
Hub	Coleridge College had set up hubs within the English, mathematics, science, modern foreign languages and design technology departments. Each hub was a classroom within a particular department with approximately 15 computers, separate from the main suites of computers within the ICT department. The computers were available for any students to use, but priority was given to those studying the hub's subject, i.e. students studying mathematics would have priority over other students who wanted to use machines in the mathematics hub.
Independent learning	Students taking responsibility for their learning by carrying out their own research (e.g. using the Internet) and preparing reports/presentations to show what they have learnt. Students have more control over the pace of their learning and the resources they use than in traditional lessons.
Inward facing	A term used by the local education authority to refer to parts of their website which could only be accessed by users connected to the local education authority intranet.

Key Skills A programme covering: communication; application of number; information technology; improving own learning; working with others; and problem solving. Students can gain accreditation in IT as a Key Skill; the government has set a target that 70–90 per cent of school leavers should be accredited in IT skills by 2002.

KS/Key Stage Key Stage: different years of primary and secondary education as follows:

Key Stage	School Year	Ages
1	1–2	5–7 years
2	3–6	8–11 years
3	7–9	12–14 years
4	10–11	15–16 years
5	12–13	17–18 years

LEA Local Education Authority: a regional body involved in the management of local state schools. There are 150 LEAs covering England; they are largely linked to geographical/administrative areas.

LSA Learning Support Assistant: an adult who assists the teacher and pupils in the classroom. Each class at Windmill Primary School had at least one LSA in addition to the teacher.

MFL Modern Foreign Languages: at Belgrove School French, Spanish and German were offered as part of the curriculum.

National Curriculum The subjects that pupils in state schools have to study. For each subject there are statutory Orders, which specify the content that teachers have to cover, although they are free to use whatever approach they wish in their lessons.
See also www.nc.uk.net/home.html

NGfL National Grid for Learning: a means of supporting lifelong learning via the Internet. The grid aims to provide information and resources for teachers, students, managers and the community.
See www.ngfl.gov.uk

NOF New Opportunities Fund: funds raised by the national lottery to support projects in education, health and the environment. One of the education projects funds ICT training for teachers and librarians.
See www.nof.org.uk/edu/edu.htm

OFSTED	Office for Standards in Education: the government agency which carries out inspections of schools and local education authorities. See www.ofsted.gov.uk

Open University	The Open University is the UK's largest university for part-time higher education, and offers distance education materials for undergraduate and postgraduate students.
See www.open.ac.uk/frames.html

Originator	A person who initiates an idea which is subsequently developed by that person and by others. There were two originators for Challenge 2000; other people subsequently became authors of some of the material for Challenge 2000.

Outward facing	A term used by the local education authority to refer to their website which could be accessed by anyone with Internet access.

Pathfinder	A local education authority given additional funding under the National Grid for Learning (NGfL) to explore new initiatives relating to supporting ICT in schools.

Picture Tel	One of the video-conferencing systems used at Belgrove School; requires connection via a PC.

Police checks	Screening checks carried out by the police to confirm that individuals who will be having access to children do not have undesirable backgrounds, such as criminal records.

PPP	Public Private Partnership (formerly Private Finance Initiative – PFI): a new way of providing ICT resources for schools by means of a contract between a private commercial company and a local education authority. The LEA in which Moorcroft was located was involved in a PPP contract for ICT. Instead of schools individually buying or leasing hardware and software, the LEA negotiated a contract with a company that could supply hardware, software, peripherals, technical support and training to its schools. Each school contributes an annual sum to participate in the scheme. The contract lasts ten years and includes scheduled replacement of hardware.

QCA	Qualifications and Curriculum Authority: the government body responsible for overseeing the content of the curriculum and its assessment in schools. See www.qca.org.uk/index.asp

Research Machines	A major UK ICT company which offers hardware, software and managed services.
Set	A method of grouping students into teaching groups according to their ability. At Belgrove, students taking GCSE French were organised into three sets; students in the two classes which formed the top set were offered the opportunity to participate in the voluntary lunchtime video-conferencing sessions.
Sixth form	Years 12 and 13 in secondary school. Students elect to study in these years as compulsory education ends at 16 years.
Specialist status	Schools which offer enhanced facilities and tuition in a particular area (such as ICT or languages) can apply for specialist status; these schools qualify for additional funding from the government, but charge no fees to students. Belgrove had specialist status as a language college.
Swift Site	One of the video-conferencing systems used at Belgrove; requires connection via a television.
The Educator	An internet-based resource for teachers: it assists teachers by allowing them to record assessments of each pupil in the class against National Curriculum Assessment criteria. Graphical analysis at class level can be provided, free of charge. It also provides links to other websites, such as those of government agencies related to education. See www.the-educator.co.uk
Thematic approach	See 'Cross-curricular'.
Travelogue	A term used within Challenge 2000 materials to describe the information that pupils have to prepare to describe/illustrate the cultural essence of a country they have 'visited' as part of their simulated journey around the world.
TMG	Target minimum grade (in formal examinations at 16+ and/or 18+).
YELLIS	Year 11 indicator system. See also www.cem.dur.ac.uk/yellis

APPENDIX I:
Research methodology

This appendix provides more detailed information about the study methodology than is presented within the main report.

An important part of any international comparative study is the adoption of the same methods and instruments for collecting data. This applies as much to qualitative research projects as to quantitative studies. For SITES M2, the International Coordinating Committee (ICC) produced guidelines for all main aspects of the study, including:

♦ a draft definition of innovative pedagogical practices using ICT

♦ composition of a national panel to agree a definition of what constituted innovative practices within the national context, and agree on the selection of schools for the case studies

♦ procedures for nominating as 'innovative' particular practices within schools

♦ instruments for data collection

♦ the structure and length of reports on each case study submitted to the ICC.

1.1 National panel

A national panel was convened to consider the definitions of innovative practices drafted by the ICC and to make any adaptations necessary for implementation in England. The panel included representatives from the following organisations:

♦ the Department for Education and Skills (DfES)

♦ the British Educational Communications and Technology Agency (BECTa)

♦ the Office for Standards in Education (OFSTED)

♦ the Qualifications and Curriculum Authority (QCA)

♦ the Teacher Training Agency (TTA)

♦ the National Association of Advisers for Computer Education (NAACE)

♦ Micros and Primary Education (MAPE)

♦ the National Foundation for Educational Research (NFER).

The nationally agreed definition of innovative practices had to be submitted to the ICC together with reasons for deviating from the draft definition. The national definition of innovative practices is shown in the next section.

1.2   School selection

The national panel discussed the draft list of innovative practices, including the definitions of 'innovative' prepared by the ICC (lettered sections a–g in section 1.2.2 below) and felt that it was comprehensive, although the practices might be better termed 'effective' rather than 'innovative' practices. The additional definition (h) was unanimously accepted by the panel as being relevant to practices in schools in England. The additional definition is relevant to both primary and secondary schools in England, the former especially since the introduction of policies requiring a focus on whole-class interactive teaching in numeracy and literacy.

The selection criteria that were approved by the national panel and applied by the research team are shown below; italicised text indicates where the panel expressed particular views concerning the draft international guidelines.

1.2.1 Selection criteria

To qualify as an innovative pedagogical practice using technology, a practice must be one:

1. In which technology plays a substantial role. Technology should not merely replace previous practices but make a significant contribution to change. These contributions should be articulated clearly. *The panel acknowledged that the existence of considerable technological resources need not necessarily be associated with pedagogical innovation. Conversely, innovative practices might be evident with relatively low levels of technological resourcing.*

2. That shows evidence of significant changes in roles of teachers and students, the goals of the curriculum, and/or the educational materials or infrastructure. This evidence might systematically document the previous practices and roles and compare them with those associated with the introduction or development of the innovation. Or the evidence might show how the practices in this classroom are significantly different from those in typical classrooms in the country. *The curriculum goals of state schools in England are guided by National Curriculum Orders which apply to students aged 5–16, which set out the content which should be covered in different subjects. However, teachers have freedom to choose the most appropriate pedagogical approaches and resources to support teaching and learning as they cover particular areas of the curriculum.*

3. That shows evidence of measurable positive student outcomes. This evidence might be formal evaluations (if such exist), quantified data that demonstrate positive change (e.g., increased achievement scores, diminished gaps in achievement between groups, increased enrolment in rigorous courses, increased graduation rates, etc.), or in-depth qualitative data, such as systematic analysis of student products compared with previous products. In general, multiple

forms of supporting evidence would make a stronger case than a single form. *There is a tension between innovative practices that have only recently been introduced, and therefore take some time before impact on students (such as achievement measures, attitudinal and/or behavioural measures) can be determined, and practices which have been in place for sufficient time to show an impact on students, but are no longer deemed innovative. Panel members commented on the role that longitudinal studies have in monitoring changes over time.*

4. That is sustainable and transferable. 'Lighthouse cases' would not qualify. These are schools or classrooms that have achieved much as a result of extraordinary resources that could not be replicated elsewhere. Although pilot projects are often used to test innovations that might be disseminated nationally, such projects should be included only if the potential for sustainability and transferability can be established. This might involve a description of how other schools or teachers could adopt the programme with a less-specialized set of resources. *The panel felt it was difficult to distinguish between 'lighthouse' and 'pilot' cases whilst projects were in the relatively early stages of development: it is often only with hindsight that it becomes clear into which category specific cases fall.*

And as a final criterion, innovative pedagogical practice using technology are those practices:

5. That are 'innovative', as defined in England.

1.2.2 'Innovative' practices

'Innovative' practices will vary according to the age of the students, the established pedagogy in the school/classroom/the resources available, but examples might include those practices that:

a) Promote active and independent learning in which students take responsibility for their own learning, set their own learning goals, create their own learning activities, and/or assess their own progress and/or the progress of other students.

b) Provide students with competencies and technological skills that allow them to search for, organize, and analyse information, and communicate and express their ideas in a variety of media forms.

c) Engage students in collaborative, project-based learning in which students work with others on complex, extended, real-world-like problems or projects.

d) Provide students with individualised instruction, customised to meet the needs of students with different entry levels, interests, or conceptual difficulties.

e) Address issues of equity for students of different genders or ethnic or social groups and/or provide access to instruction or information for students who would not have access otherwise because of geographic or socio-economic reasons.

f) 'Break down the walls' of the classroom – for example, by extending the school day, changing the organisation of the class, or involving other people (such as parents, scientists, or business professionals) in the education process.

g) Improve social cohesiveness and understanding by having students interact with groups and cultures that they would not interact with otherwise.

h) Make effective use of demonstration/presentation aspects of technology in whole-class teaching.

1.2.3 The school selection process

This section describes the process by which schools were selected to participate in the study in England; similar procedures were adopted in other countries so as to conform with the international study guidelines prepared by the ICC.

The research team gathered data about schools which may have had innovative pedagogical practices involving ICT. The crucial factors stipulated by the ICC for a particular practice to be considered 'innovative' were as follows:

♦ the practice must involve changed roles for teachers

♦ the practice must involve changed roles for students

♦ there must be evidence of a beneficial impact on students (in terms of achievement, attitudes, motivation, attendance and/or behaviour)

♦ the practice must be sustainable over time

♦ the practice must be transferable to other classes/schools

♦ the practice must involve ICT.

Importantly, the emphasis was *not* on innovative technology, but innovative practices that involved new or changed roles for teachers and pupils, and in which ICT played a part. A total of six schools (three primary and three secondary) with innovations was required for the national research. The strategies used to identify suitable schools included:

a. Schools listed on the European Network of Innovative Schools (ENIS) were contacted and asked if they had suitable innovations currently in place and would be willing to participate in the research.

b. The British Educational Communications and Technology Agency (BECTa) was asked to recommend some primary and secondary schools which their own records showed as having innovative pedagogical practices.

c. Some additional schools were known to the research team and/or the national panel (e.g. as award-winners and through previous involvement) and were also contacted as in (a) above.

Preliminary contacts with the schools outlined the study requirements and explained what the case studies would involve. Schools that were willing to participate were asked to describe a pedagogical approach being used in at least one class which they thought was innovative. This resulted in a longlist of 12 secondary school and ten primary school innovations.

Guidelines prepared by the ICC instructed national research teams to exclude 'lighthouse cases': schools which had exceptional levels of resources or facilities that were unlikely to be attainable by typical schools within the country. In addition, the national panel decided to exclude independent schools and to consider overall school performance as a criterion for selection. Consequently, performance data and OFSTED reports were collated for schools on the long-list. The panel decided that, in order to be considered for participation, schools should have performance data[1] above the local and/or national averages (or show evidence of ongoing improvements in performance) and a favourable OFSTED report. Subsequently, the panel excluded a small number of schools on the following bases:

♦ not representative of typical schools in England (e.g. schools that had adopted practices such as a four-term year)

♦ involvement in other major government-funded research projects.

A further consideration was that another major international research study was also focusing on ICT in schools. The Centre for Educational Research and Innovation (CERI) of the Organisation for Economic Co-operation and Development (OECD) had established a study into whole-school reform supported by ICT. The DfES had sponsored national participation in this study. Thus, two international research projects were focusing on ICT in schools and collecting data at a similar time: one (the IEA's SITES) focused on innovative pedagogical practices at classroom level, the other (the OECD study) focused on whole-school reform supported by ICT. In order to achieve economies of effort in data collection, the national panel decided to select three schools for participation in both the SITES and OECD studies, and three further schools for SITES only.

Finally, the panel identified a shortlist of schools which met the criteria stated above, and represented different geographical areas and also different types of innovative practice. Each short-listed school was visited by one or more members of the research team to assess the suitability of the innovation (and, where applicable, the suitability of the whole-school reform for inclusion within the OECD research) and to explain in more detail the data-collection process. After confirming the suitability of the innovation in each school, the research team prepared a formal nomination of the pedagogical practice to the ICC: all nominations were scrutinised by members of the ICC to ensure the practice fulfilled the study requirements for an 'innovation'.

Eight nominations for innovative practices were submitted by the research team in England and six were accepted by the ICC. Case studies were subsequently carried out in three primary schools and three secondary schools, as shown in Table 1 below.

---

[1] Performance data included National Curriculum assessment at the end of Key Stage 2 and GCSE results at the end of Key Stage 4.

Table A1.2.1: Location of schools selected for the SITES and OECD studies

School	Location
Primary 1	south west (SITES only)
Primary 2	north midlands (SITES and OECD)
Primary 3	west midlands (SITES only)
Secondary 1	south east (SITES and OECD)
Secondary 2	north midlands (SITES and OECD)
Secondary 3	north east (SITES only)

Within the three schools used for both the SITES and OECD studies, in one case the same aspect of school practice was used for both studies, and in the other two schools different aspects were the focus for the SITES and OECD studies respectively.

1.3　Data collection

A pilot study was carried out in the summer term 2000. The pilot study provided an opportunity to use the draft instruments, and allowed national research teams to submit to the ICC comments and suggestions for revisions to the instruments on the basis of their experiences in schools. The data collection for the main study in England took place between November 2000 and May 2001.

In each school, researchers collected data over a period of five days by means of:

- interviews with headteachers and ICT coordinators/heads of ICT;

- interviews with teachers using the innovative practice and with others who were not;

- focus groups with pupils in the innovative classes, and parents of some of these pupils;

- observations of sessions in which the innovative practices were used;

- interviews with LEA advisers;

- analysis of school documents, such as school prospectuses and ICT policies.

In addition, the headteacher and the head of ICT/ICT coordinator in each school were asked to complete a questionnaire about ICT within the school: the data from all the completed surveys will be analysed by the ICC and presented in an international report on the study. In accordance with the international guidelines, two researchers were present for all interviews and observations, and all interviews were recorded.

1.4 Data analysis and reporting

The data collected from each school were analysed by the research team: a main part of the analysis involved identifying where there were substantive changes in the roles of both teachers and students (as compared with their previous practices) and considering the role that ICT played in supporting these changed roles. The research team had to submit to the ICC evidence collected from several different sources in support of any statement or claims as part of the process of quality control. The structure for the case reports was provided by the ICC and applied to the reports submitted by all national research teams. The full case reports on the six schools studied in England will be available, together with those from other participating countries (in English language) via the study website (http://sitesm2.org).

APPENDIX II:

A sample email from the innovation teacher to his class at Windmill Primary School

Hi all,

As you will have realised there is a new way to do your mental arithmetic today. If you log back into the maths you can view done assignments. This will show you the marks that you got. If you got any wrong see if you can work out where you went wrong.

When you have done your mental arithmetic you need to get out your crossword and continue designing it. We shall talk about designing it on the computer and working out clues in a while. We are also going to be writing a short story today.

Remember that you can do:

1. The newspaper work that I have given you
2. Book reviews
3. The science investigation write-ups
4. History work
5. Homework
6. Science quiz

And lots, lots more!

(Innovation teacher)

APPENDIX III:

The BITC evaluation of the epals project: pupils' self-ratings on skills and attitudes before and after the project at Woodford Junior School.

The SITES research team is grateful to the coordinator at Business in the Community for permission to reproduce these results. The BITC evaluation was designed, organised and analysed by the BITC coordinator.

Figure 1: Pupils' self-ratings on 'Skills in using a computer'

Figure 2: Pupils' self-ratings on 'Ability to use email'

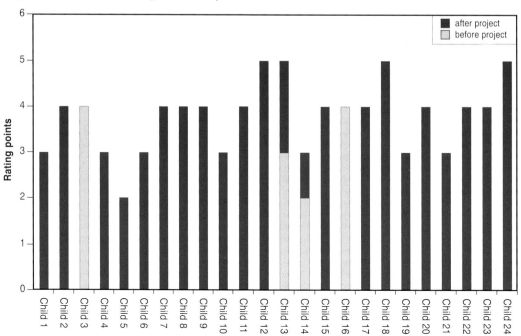

Figure 3: Pupils' self-ratings on 'Ability at finding information from the internet'

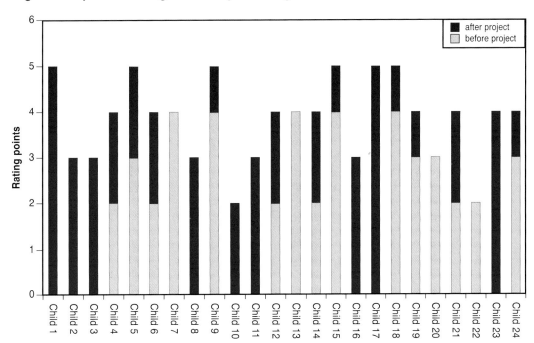

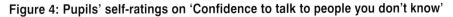

Figure 4: Pupils' self-ratings on 'Confidence to talk to people you don't know'

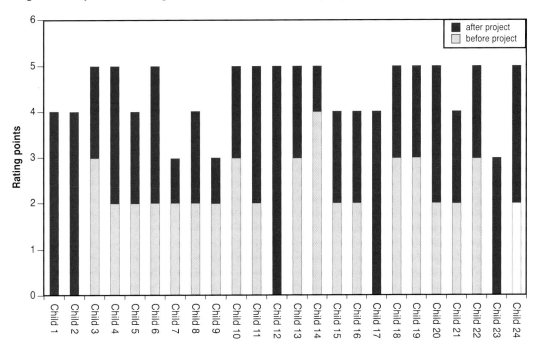

Figure 5: Pupils' self-ratings on 'Ability to write so anyone can understand you'

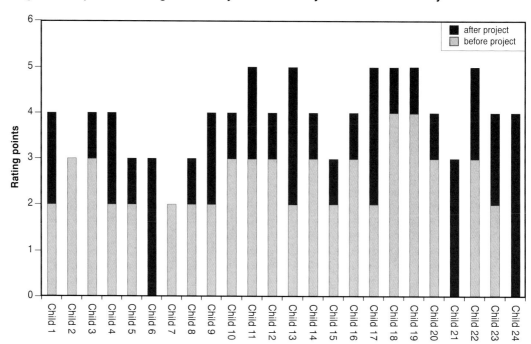

Figure 6: Pupils' self-ratings on 'Knowledge about what people do at work'

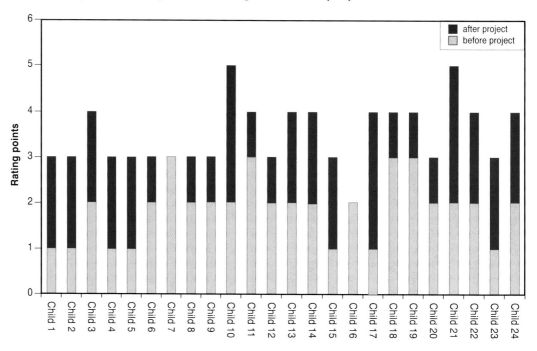

Figure 7: Pupils' self-ratings on 'Ambitions for your own ability to earn a living in the future'

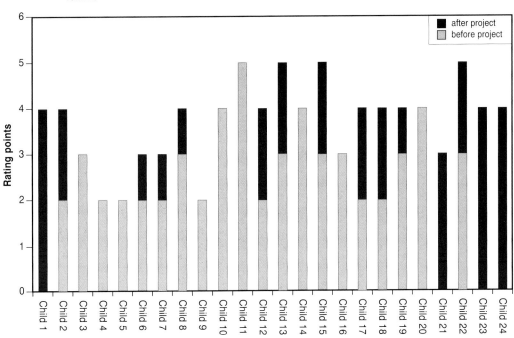

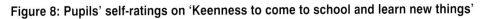

Figure 8: Pupils' self-ratings on 'Keenness to come to school and learn new things'

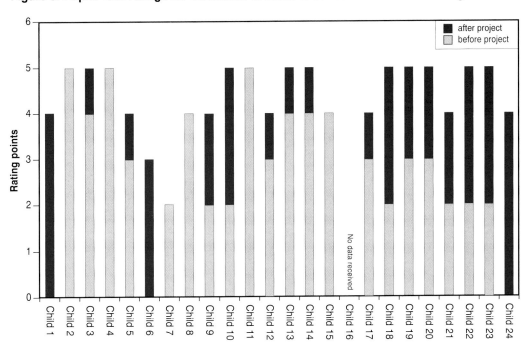

Figure 9: Difference in each pupil's self-ratings before and after epals

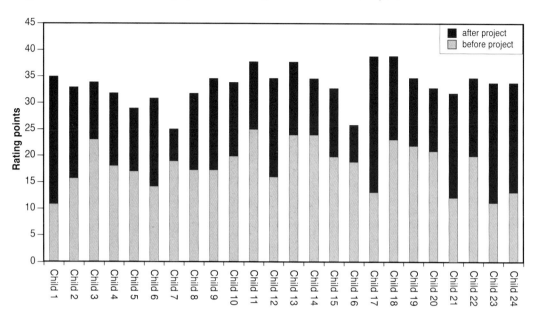

Figure 10: Difference in all pupils' self-ratings for different skills

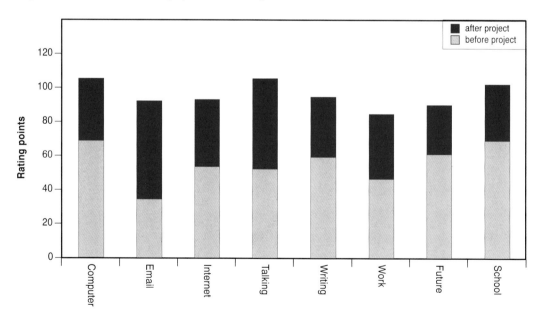

APPENDIX IV:
One of the monthly 'stages' in Challenge 2000 used at Moorcroft Primary School

4th stage

 Mission Control   Main page   Next slide ▶

This challenge is by WEST MIDLANDS
Ambulance Service
NHS TRUST

Up, Up and Away
- Go East
brave traveller!

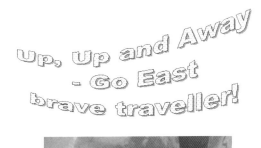

Look at the image - you are crossing the largest landlocked sea in the World - flying South-East.
a) name the sea. *(50 km)*
b) how many countries border this sea? *(50 km)*
c) list them clockwise – starting with the country you are leaving. *(100 km)*

The World's Longest River
Look left - it's the World's longest river. It ends in a delta which has been compared with a flower.
a) the river is the ....*(50 km)*
b) the flower is the ....*(50 km)*

The balloon flies on towards another wet land mark – found in **Exodus 13: Verses 17-22.** Name it. *(50 km)*

This area is visited by thousands of divers every year. They are attracted by the wonderful sea life and its coral reefs. It's tempting to stop and take a swim but there is no time. The balloon is heading across an ancient land famous for many things including 1001 nocturnal tales.

Previous slide   Mission Control   Main page   Next slide

Mayday!   Mayday!   Mayday!

Do not panic! Stay calm!

You must listen carefully to the symptoms of the illness.

You will have to list them or try to remember them.

Next, match the symptoms to the illness – then take action – quickly, but calmly. A life may be at risk here.

a) What was the illness you diagnosed?

b) What action did you take?

Making the correct decisions is worth *500 km.*

Press the refresh button to hear the message again

CLICK FOR HELP

Previous slide Mission Control Main page Next slide

A HOLY CITY

This is one of the most important religious cities in the World. At its centre you will find 'The Kaaba'

What is the Kaaba? *(50 km)*

You might be allowed to visit this city – but only if you are a member of which religion? *(50 km)*

What am I?

I go from right to left. I am one of 18 or 28 when mixed.

I have no capital. *(50 km)*

امی = l+م+م+ی

Above is the name of someone close to you – who is it?
(100 km)

Welcome to the World's largest sand desert and the hottest place on the planet. You must survive in these harsh conditions. Good luck – you will need it!

What is this desert called? *(50 km)*

Previous slide

 Mission Control

 Main page

 Next slide

You are flying across one of the most dangerous environments in the World. You are flying east. Before you attempt the crossing – you must:

a) Learn at least 5 survival skills – should your balloon be forced to land. What are the 3 GOLDEN RULES OF SURVIVAL? *(200 km)*

b) Fill this rucksack with equipment needed to survive. Choose carefully! (Add rules / skills list and equipment to Travelogue) Get expert advice! (Email *an expert? 500 km bonus)*

c) What do these people have in common: Jamie Clarke, Bruce Kirkby, Leigh Clarke and Wilfred Thesiger? Which is the odd one out *(100 km)*

Previous slide   Mission Control   Main page   Next slide

Find a lost city!

On the left you will find a satellite image of a great city – lost for hundreds of years beneath the sands. This was a very wealthy city – important for trading a range of valuable goods – but one – especially, a sweet smelling substance which was as valuable as gold (luban in Arabic).

The city was also known as Iram in two of the World's great books.

a) Name the lost city. (*100 km*)

b) Name the substance as valuable as gold. (*100 km*)

These clues will lead you to one of the World's great collection of stories. A collection of tales to save a young girl's life!
There is a link between these tales and:
    a) The road that links London to Leeds
    b) What a paramedic calls a heart attack

        What is the link? (*200 km*)
        Clue – Think like a Roman!

Meet **Abu Bakr al - Razi** - a great man.

What does he have in common with these other people?
a) Ibn al-Nafis
b) Ibn Sina

These people made an important contribution in the field of ... (*100 km*)

Previous slide   Mission Control   Main page

Touchdown Warning!

Congratulations!

You have made it across the desert ... What a relief! But now you have to land. Take care though, there are strong cross-winds that may make landing difficult!

Time to land – near the Tropic of Cancer!

You are about to land near the capital city of this country. It is a sea port where you will find a very impressive palace. Take your time and have a good look around, and try to capture the 'magic' of this place for your journey travelogue.

Remember...
a) *Record all your answers – and where you found them!*
b) *Discuss strategies for solving the problems with other groups (groups in other countries.. perhaps!)*
c) *Complete the practical task set below... There is a special prize for completing the task.*

DISASTER!   DISASTER!   DISASTER!

Your balloon has crashed heavily and one of your team has broken their femur.

    a) who will you contact for help? *(50 km)*

    b) where will your team member be treated? *(50 km)*

You will have to treat the patient until help arrives. To treat a broken femur you will need 7 triangular bandages and a splint.

Find out what you need to do next.

When you have treated 'the patient' take a digital photograph and email it to:

bc.wmas.oman@lineone.net

There is a class prize for the best entry
– a visit to the air ambulance base at RAF Cosford.

WOW! – what a prize!

Good luck!

APPENDIX V:
The use of the student tracking database in Highgrove High School

The school has a computer database for storing information about student acheivement.

Key stage	Year group	Activity	Key people	Technical overview
3	7	Enter data from Y6 NCA; administer NFER CAT tests; enter data and report CAT results to parents; enter achievement and effort grades for all subjects – report these to parents as interim and end-of-year reports.	Head of Year 7; subject coordinators; Head of KS3	Head of KS3/ lower school
	8	Enter achievement and effort grades for all subjects – report these to parents as interim and end-of-year reports.	Head of Year 8; subject coordinators; Head of KS3	
	9	Administer NFER CAT tests; enter data and report CAT results to parents; enter achievement and effort grades for all subjects – report these to parents as interim and end-of-year reports; administer NCA and report to parents and government (results must be published).	Head of Year 9; subject coordinators; Head of KS3	
4	10	Administer YELLIS tests. Enter achievement and effort grades for all subjects – report these to parents as interim and end-of-year reports; set TMGs for GCSEs based on YELLIS. Report YELLIS results to parents.	Head of Year 10; subject coordinators; Head of KS4	Value Added Coordinor
	11	Enter achievement and effort grades for all subjects – report these to parents as interim and end-of-year reports; administer GCSEs (16+ accreditation) and report to government (results must be published).	Head of Year 11; subject coordinators; Head of KS4	
5	12	Administer ALIS tests. Set TMGs for A/AS/VCE courses based on ALIS; enter achievement and effort grades for all subjects – report these to parents each term and in end-of-year reports. Give ALIS feedback to students and parents, highlighting significance of results.	Head of Year 12; Head of KS5; Director of sixth form studies	Head of ICT
	13	Set TMGs for A/AS/VCE courses based on past performance and higher education entry requirements; enter achievement and effort grades for all subjects – report these to parents each term and in end-of-year reports; administer A/AS/VCE exams and report to government (results must be published).	Head of Year 13; Head of KS5; Director of sixth form studies	

APPENDIX VI:

Typical questions for one of the weekly Year 11 video-conferencing sessions at Belgrove High School

Nom d'élève francais _____

Nom d'élève anglais _____

La Santé

1. Qu'est-ce que tu aimes manger?

2. Que'est-ce que tu n'aimes pas manger?

3. Est-ce que tu manges assez de légumes?

4. Est-ce que tu manges de la viande?

5. Tu bois de l'alcool?

6. A quelle heure te couche-tu le weekend?

7. Et pendant la semaine?

8. Qu'est-ce que tu fais comme sport?

9. Es-tu en bonne forme?

10. Est-ce que la drogue est un problème pour les jeunes dans la ville?

APPENDIX VII:

Quantitative evidence from other research concerning the impact of video-conferencing on student achievement in Year 11 at Belgrove High School

Belgrove High School was keen to determine whether or not the innovation had a measurable impact on student achievement, and had therefore invited the University of Durham to carry out analyses of the differences between predicted and actual achievement in formal examinations at 16+ (General Certificate of Secondary Education – GCSE). A second study had been set up using an experimental group design (an experimental group and a matched control group). The SITES research team would like to acknowledge the information collected and analysed by other teams (see below), and made available to them by the school.

Data collected and analysed by the University of Durham showed that students who had participated in foreign language courses which involved considerable use of ICT (including video-conferencing sessions) achieved grades higher than were predicted in the formal French examination (GCSE). The results achieved by the 1997 cohort of GCSE students at Belgrove High School (116 entrants for GSCE French) were compared with 48,000 students in other schools throughout England. The data had been collected and were analysed within the Year 11 Indicator System (the YELLIS project) which predicts students' grades in GCSE examinations (see http://cem.dur.ac.uk/yellis). The report noted '...*that achievement was more than a grade higher, on average, than statistically predicted.*' The school's own records of students' predicted and achieved grades showed that this positive impact on student achievement had been maintained for four years.

The school had also collaborated with a researcher from the University of Durham's Curriculum Evaluation and Management Centre in an attempt to determine specifically the effects of video-conferencing (as opposed to an ICT-rich learning environment which included video-conferencing) on Year 11 students' GCSE grades in French; this focused on the 1999–2000 cohort of students. The project collected and analysed data relating to 20 students in a treatment group (ten weekly sessions of video-conferencing) and 21 students in a control group (no video-conferencing). After excluding the results for one student who did not speak during the oral examination, the analysis showed that the students who had taken part in the video-conferencing sessions achieved higher scores for the speaking component of the GCSE examination; this difference was statistically significant ($p=0.01$). However, as the report noted, it would be unwise to draw conclusions from these data, as the analysis was based on a very small sample and other factors (such as student motivation) might have affected the results.